SERMONS

FROM THE

GREEN LEATHER CHAIR

Amazing Stories, Life Lessons

&

Wisdom

Thomas A. Cook

Copyright © 2023 by Thomas A. Cook

All rights reserved.

No portion of this book may be reproduced in any form without written permission from the publisher or author, except as permitted by U.S. copyright law.

Contents

Acknowledgments	VI
Forward	VII
Preface	IX
The Air Drop	1
Back to the Start and Into the World	9
The Parkridge House	11
Lessons from the Silver Piggy Bank	13
My Dog Topper	17
Mom and Self-Reliance	23
Sermons from the Green Leather Chair	25
The M-80	29
Quip: Do you know right from wrong? Part one	33
Jack	35
My Friend Chris King	37
Rats for Mrs. Vest	39
Kool-Aid Stand	41
My Bank	43

Quip: Never Be Classed	45
Saint Robert School	47
Quip: You wouldn't care so much what people thought of you if you knew how little they did – don't worry about it.	51
Gold Doorknob Theory	53
Quip: WORK, WORK, WORK	55
SOS	57
Quip: Listen, Listen: Listen to the other guy and you will know what he knows and what you know.	59
Judo Lessons	61
Quip: Don't talk about it – do it	63
The Skateboard Dummy	65
Quip: Do you know right from wrong? Part 2: The Risk Area	67
Do You Want to Buy Some Stock?	69
Fast Cars, Muscle Cars	71
Early Primitive Inklings	73
Quip: Class is hard to describe, but you know it when you see it.	75
Quip: I never met a man I didn't like, if I took the time to know him. But I had a choice of who I took the time with.	77
School Change	79
Rick and Chocolate	81
Quip: Right from Wrong, Part 3: Mitigating the Risk	83
Getting Set for Life: Approval, Recognition, and Encouragement	87
Christian Brothers School	89
Quip: Right from Wrong, Part 4: I Can't Be with You	91

Quip: What if and then what?	93
Cadillac Rabbit Chasing	95
Land Lease	97
Quip: Be Good	101
Cook-King Casinos	103
The 100-Horse Merc	107
Box of Dirt	109
One of My Own Quips: Tomorrow Will be a Better Day	113
Quip: Take care of yourself and you will take care of everyone around you.	117
Becoming an Adult	119
The Army Story	121
I Call Them Godfather Moments	135
Life is Not Always Fair	137
Expensive Blaze	143
The Sierra Trek	145
Quip: It's never quite as good or quite as bad as you really think it is.	149
Proper Way to Throw a Punch	151
Quip: WORK, WORK, WORK (revisited)	157
New Porsche	159
Struggles and Survival	161
My Friend Steve Crowle	165
Benson Lake Revisited	167
Slow Road	171
Broken Back	173
Call of the Wild	175

Wants and Needs	181
Following Tracks	183
The Benson Bear	185
My Children	187
Your Tracks	191
My Brother's Death	193
Clear the Office	197
Followed His Path	199
Get Mad and You Lose	203
Life Lessons Learned: Make the Deal and Move On	205
You're Picking on the Wrong Motherfucker Tonight	207
Balance Needed	209
The General	211
Every Form of Refuge Has Its Price	213
After-Work Chats	217
Be Careful What You Wish For	219
Quip: Tip of My Finger	221
Never Going to Get Angry Again	223
Life Regrets	225
A Significant Dream	227
Pray for a Parking Space	229
Thing to Ponder	231
The Patch	235
Stress	237
Attitude	239
Joys of Teaching	241

Melt My Heart	245
Finale	249
Reviews	255

Acknowledgments

I want to thank Dave Perrault for his constant urging. Thanks to my wife Sandy for her love, help, patience and support in producing the book. Also, much thanks to my editor Meredith Linden, for all her inspirational help. The stories were the easy part of this book; the rest of the book was difficult and I could not have done it without Meredith's guidance, direction, and friendship: priceless.

FORWARD

Knowing Tom and his stories but not having read his book yet, I offer the following:

You are about to traverse the lifetime brilliance of one Thomas Cook, as only he can describe it: actual events and his musings. You will be truly rewarded, and at times amazed, as you read his book. You may think, "He did what? You are kidding me. He said that? Really? How did he survive this long?"

I have known Tom since 1988, if memory serves. He is a friend, a back-country guru, an avid duck hunter, a man of incredible theoretical and practical foresight, as well as having been my client. In each of those moments when I was engaged or involved with Tom about "something," he never ceased to amaze. You are about to enjoy that "amazement."

You will experience in your mind's eye Tom as he grew up in Sacramento, California as a benevolent prankster in his own mind and a notorious one in his parents' minds, for sure. How he survived his teen years is a mystery for you, the reader, to solve.

Then you will wander over the highs and lows of Tom's adult life, through his profession as a contractor (the good, the bad and the ugly), his societal happenings, his teachings to all age groups about his love for and interaction with the gifts of nature and its outdoor blessings (such as finding wild asparagus along the American River), survival skills and his travels in the Sierras of California, the deserts of Arizona, the beaches of Hawaii, and the ski slopes of Colorado.

I hope Tom sneaks into this book his political aspirations, never achieved, but with an amazing clarity of purpose that he would have pursued for the good of all humankind. What a governor of California he would have been, or a US President.

In closing, I am confident you will read this book not once, but twice. I am equally confident you will pass the book on to your friends and family for their enjoyment. You may even consider inviting Tom to your community/neighborhood or book club for a book signing and to seek more insight from this amazing adventurer.

David Perrault

PREFACE

My friend Dave Perault had been after me for over twenty years to write down my stories that his son Bryan named the Benson Lake Chronicles on one of our many trips into Benson Lake. The original title of this book was going to be The Benson Lake Chronicles: My Stories, but when adding in my life to the stories, the title changed to the Sermons from the Green Leather Chair. So, this book is a combination of my stories (Benson Lake Chronicles) and my life and relationship with my dad (Sermons from the Green Leather Chair).

Because of Dave's continual urging, I went backpacking into Benson Lake with my friends Dave Gustafson, Mike Nolasco and Roger Haaf with a recorder to record my stories. Then I had them transcribed and sent them to an editor that my wife Sandy found for me. Meredith went through about 90% of it and said, "I can see from the stories, and reading between the lines the kind of life you have lived and you need to put it in the book." Knowing my history, I said, "Oh, I don't know about that." I thought to myself, "Do I really want to disclose all my missteps, mistakes, faults, and behavior?" She told me calmly that she understood but for it to be a book, it needed connective tissue and if that wasn't something I wanted to do, she wouldn't be able to help me.

I wasn't listening. Many times in life, we misperceive things and I thought at first that she was dropping the project and running away from me, when in fact she was running right at me. I just didn't recognize it.

Shaken but not deterred, I put the stories in a binder and took them on our vacation to Hawaii to read around the pool. While there, I meet a lady from Kentucky, Gail Babb, at the smoking bench at the Kanapalli Ali'i in Maui, and over the next 5 days, we became friends.

The first time we met, I had told my wife I was going down to the smoking bench. After 45 minutes my phone rang. I picked it up and Sandy said, "Where are you?" I said I am at the smoking bench, talking with Gail and I will be up in a couple minutes. When I got back to the room, Sandy said, "You know, you have been gone for almost an hour and who is Gail?" Later that day, I introduced Sandy to my new friend Gail and her husband Dave.

Knowing Gail was an avid reader, on her last day, I asked her if she wanted to read the stories. She did, finishing it just in time to pack and catch their plane home. She wrote on the last page "amazing life." But I did not get a chance to talk with her. Some weeks later, I texted her and asked if she had any ideas on how I might make this into a book rather than just a bunch of stories and to let me know of a good time to call. When I called, she said, "Oh that's easy." I said, "Really?" She said, "Oh yeah, who are you and where did you come from?" (It's been years since that meeting and we are still in touch with each other.)

This then made it clear that Meredith was right as usual and was running right at me. I call Gail "my little angel" for getting me off the dime to at least give it a try. But at the time, I was still very hesitant and scared to dig in, dig up and reveal all of the mistakes, missteps, faults and failures in my life. It has been one of the hardest things I have tried to do and has been years and years in the journey. Some of it was not fun due to dealing with all of the negative things and emotions that occurred. It impacted life perceptions and relationships, and that was tough to get through. Good and bad, it helped me understand my part in things, helped me have a better understanding of the impacts of life events. I think I have learned a lot about myself, but in the book, I did not dwell or detail the negative details. In the process even the toughest areas turned into a joy overall because of all that was revealed in the process.

Over the many years of working on this book, I was asked several times, "Why are you writing this book?" I could not answer the question. My first thought was the stories for my friends, then there was the addition of my life for myself, as suggested by Meredith. But still the question remained, "Why and who are you writing this for?" I thought to myself, "I am writing this for my close friends and for my family of people and acquaintances at my primitive skills gatherings who may have heard some of my stories around the fire and know who I am but do not know my life. I wanted to share it with them. I then realized I was writing this for all people because I want to share my stories and life's journey, but, more importantly, I wanted to pass on the wisdom and life lessons I got from my dad.

Although out of sequence, I begin with the "AIR DROP" to introduce you to Benson Lake because of the importance it had in my life; it was the turning point into a new and different life. It was the end of my Tomfooleries because after years of struggling, I had finally stopped drinking and doing cocaine and was on a very slow path to recovering and discovering a different way of life.

The Air Drop

Our family had a cabin on Highway 50 just above Camp Sacramento at Sayles Canyon Tract. We went every summer from the time I could crawl. I had heard my dad's stories about Desolation Valley, which was on the other side of the mountain in front of the cabin we had. When I was 12, I bought a canvas knapsack from the Army Surplus Store and announced to my mom that I was going backpacking into Desolation Valley for three days. I was never a Boy Scout, had no camping experience, but I was determined to go to Desolation Valley. My mom said it would be okay as long as I took a friend; so, I invited my friend Steve Crowle. We arrived at Echo Lake and took the water taxi called the "Why Walk," which cuts two and a half miles off the hike by crossing upper and lower Echo Lake by boat. From there, my mom walked us in one mile into Tamarack Lake so she would know where we were, then she left us there and walked back out.

We spent the next three days in a Tom Sawyer-like adventure. It was neat to be out in the wilderness free from parents and the world. During those three days, we fished, hiked to several other lakes. Because of my woodcraft books, we pretended we were mountain men and made a rock oven to cook our fish. We made a lean-to shelter with a long fire out in front that also had a flat rock cooking stone. We wondered about the Indians that lived here; what did they eat, how did they hunt and fish, how did they manage to live?

THOMAS A. COOK

I was an avid backpacker throughout Desolation Valley up until I was about 20 years old when career, marriage and children took priority, and I didn't backpack, except for a few trips until I was 30 when Steve Crowle invited me to go on the 1977 Lung Association Sierra Trek. The trip with a group of 25 hikers went from Kennedy Meadows to the floor of Yosemite Valley in nine and a half days. The hike was about 110 miles and at mid-point of the trek, we camped at a lake called Benson Lake.

Benson Lake is located in the middle of the Yosemite Park boundaries. It is 39 miles north of Tuolumne and 40 miles from Sonora pass and Hetch Hetchy Reservoir. This beautiful lake sits in a hole at about 8,000 feet. It has a half-mile crescent-shaped white sand beach on the north end and large meadow behind the beach. The lake is about a half-mile wide and one mile long. As you look out over the lake towards the south, to your right is Piute Peak at 11,900 feet and to your left is Volunteer Peak at 10,400 feet, which turns lavender at sunset. Seavey Pass is behind you at 9,600 feet, which is the Pacific Crest Trail used to get into Benson.

Our group arrived in late July, which is very early for backpack season in the high country. The meadow was full of water due to the heavy spring runoff that year. Benson Lake has a narrow rock drain at the downstream end of the lake that will not handle all the runoff. During the spring, the water level in the lake rises and floods the much of the beach and meadow behind the beach. Because of the high water level, the fishing at the inlet between the lake and the meadow was like being at a trout farm. After spending the night, Steve, Dave Gustafson and I were assigned rear guard duty for our group of 25 trekkers hiking over to Benson Pass and into Matterhorn Canyon, another 11-mile day. We were able to stay on the beach until about 11:00. Rear guard was a safety measure to make sure no one fell behind or had an injury.

Before heading out on the day's trek, I was sitting on the beach looking out over the lake. It was a misty morning and a double rainbow appeared, flying over the top of Piute Peak and landing directly in front of me in the lake. Just amazing. So, we finished the trek and vowed to find a shorter route to that lake and return and do it in style with good food and a raft for fishing.

SERMONS FROM THE GREEN LEATHER CHAIR

Benson Lake is such a magical place in nature. It has towering peaks that change color, a white sand beach, crystal clear water with great fishing, both lake and stream. We wanted to go back and spend a week, but we wanted to have good food and equipment and a raft for fishing and knew we could not pack it in, about five years later, John, a friend from AA and a Vietnam pilot, said he could do the air drop I had been dreaming about. I called Steve and Dave and planned the air drop into Benson Lake. Due to the prevalent winds at Benson, we didn't want to use a parachute. Instead, we decided to free drop our stuff from a plane.

I packed two duffle bags that weighed about 90 pounds each. The first bag contained a Styrofoam ice chest, a two-man raft, four fuel bottles, a three-pound slab of bacon, a Coleman oven and an alloyed hatchet. The second bag had another Styrofoam ice chest packed with more frozen goods, a sleeping bag stuff sack full of smaller bags (bags of flour, bags of pancake mix, bags of oatmeal, etc.), carton of my cigarettes, cooking oil, syrup, peanut butter and jelly and an Army shovel. Understand that the Styrofoam ice chests had been frozen in a solid block of ice and wrapped in duct tape.

I arranged with John, the pilot, to fly the plane and deliver our goods on Monday morning at 10:00. Late afternoon the Friday before, Steve, Dave and I headed into Benson from the Twin Lakes trailhead, 22 miles from Benson Lake. Getting a late start, we camped above Barney Lake the first night. The next day, we arrived at the cutoff: one trail goes to Snow Lake and the other goes to Peeler Lake. Dave, whom we called Rocket Man, was always out in front of us. The original plan was to go to Snow Lake, but Steve wasn't feeling very well and it's shorter to go to Peeler. So, we figured we'd just meet Dave on the other side of the mountain at the Rock Island trail junction. To make a long story short, we ditched Dave. He couldn't figure out where we were and went all the way back to Twin Lakes trying to find us; we had gone around him. Dave was not at Benson when the air drop took place, and it took us 10 years to apologize to him for ditching him.

Steve and I arrived at Benson Lake in the afternoon Sunday and set up our camp spot that evening as the sun was just starting to go down. Steve and I were out on the beach fishing when a plane came by on the right-hand side, going south. Surprised, I looked at it. The plane wasn't supposed to be there until the next morning at 10:00, and we hadn't even laid out the target in the meadow yet. So the plane disappeared, and we continued fishing. About five minutes later, that plane showed up again, coming down the east side of the lake hugging the cliffs. Now, you have to understand, as he was coming in, he had Volunteer Peak on his right wing and Seavey Pass directly in front of him. On the other side of the lake is Piute Peak and the only opening was out to the south. My Vietnam pilot friend only had about three-quarters of a mile to make that turn and drop low enough in elevation to free drop the bags. There is nothing but sheer granite rock walls all the way around the lake.

The plane was down fairly low. Steve asked, "When was he supposed to come?" I said, "Well, tomorrow at 10:00." He said, "Well, what color is the plane supposed to be?" And I said, "It's supposed to be red and white." He said, "Well That plane is red and white." And with that, the plane went into a WWII dive maneuver, just tipped on its side with the wing parallel to the cliff face. He dove into the valley; the plane was just screaming down in through that canyon and the sound of his straining engine was reverberating and roaring off those granite cliffs. It sounded like Pearl Harbor was about to start. As he went around, he made that tight turn up against Seavey Pass and to the side of Piute Peak where he dropped out a small test bag and disappeared heading south. Four or five minutes later, he came again flying along the east side of the lake; just before the end of the lake, he only had three-quarters of a mile of meadow and trees before the granite face to make a turn. Again, he put that plane into a steep dive and came roaring into the canyon. The noise was extremely loud echoing off the surrounding mountains. We didn't think there were many people at Benson, but I tell you, people started coming out of the woodwork. You know, there are people all over the place. The Sierra Club was not happy with us.

As he came around, out dropped the first 90-lb. bag and Steve was running around under the falling bag. I said, "For God's sake, don't catch it." You know, he was right underneath that thing.

The bag came down a perfect hit in the meadow a made a huge "whap!" It must have gone six or eight inches into the soft dirt. After the initial impact, the bag popped out of that hole and flew another 30 yards. It smacked hard again, as the ice chest ejected from the duffle bag with a "Puff." Then the three-pound package of bacon rolled up to within three feet of somebody's tent on the beach. And off went the plane. Everything in the bag was intact.

By this time, darkness was setting in, as it was almost sunset. Five minutes went by, and the plane came again, roaring into the canyon. The pilot got the second bag out just a little bit late; it flew into a grove of trees and started to come apart at about 100 feet. You could hear it going through the forest. "Crash, boom, bang." I mean, it was a wreck. There was stuff all over the place. The pork chops had been deboned, jelly was dripping from the tree branches and hamburger was embedded in the bark. The Army shovel was stuck in the tree like it was an arrow, but my cigarettes, they were perfect. They were scattered all over the place, and not a dent in them. And when I opened them, the foil was fine, but when I tried to light one, it was un-smokeable because of a thousand fractures in the paper.

At dark, we were in the forest with flashlights and we actually collected most everything that was in that bag and lost only maybe 10% of what was in it. The bags inside bags all had little holes in them. I spent about three hours that night reorganizing all the parts and pieces of it. Most of the damage was to our oils, syrup and peanut butter and jelly plastic containers. They splayed open like banana peels and all was lost.

In the first bag, the Coleman oven was fine. The fuel bottles had little dents in the top of the neck, probably caused when the oven smashed into the fuel bottles upon ground impact. All four fuel bottles had an exact bend in them that was similar to the bend in the little alloyed hatchet. It had a little kink instead of being straight; and there was a 30-degree bend on the head portion of the hatchet. We had a lot of good food so we did a lot of trading with people on the beach. Two young men had guitars with them and we fed them good food and they played good music. I also traded with them for cigarette papers and rolled my cigarettes up in them.

In the middle of the beach was a group of three large trees; we set up our camp there, constructed a lean-to and built shelves in one particular tree, giving us a sophisticated camp. We had a two-man raft and we set up a Coleman oven on the fire. We had collected log rounds for seating. Steve was a real fisherman, so the first thing he did was blow up the raft and get out on the lake. Dave finally arrived early afternoon that next day and went fishing with Steve. Later, I was just sitting in camp by myself and a guy named R.J. Sacore, a long, tall, lanky kid at the time, came by camp and said, "Do you have any hot water?" I said, "No. I don't have any hot water but I have some coffee. Sit down and have a cup of coffee."

R.J. sat down and scanned the camp. "Nice camp," he said, then asked, "How did you get this stuff in here?" Because of the commotion of the air drop the day before, we did not want to let anyone else know. I told him, "We packed it in." He said, "You packed it in? A Coleman oven, you packed it in?" I said, "Yeah, we packed it in."

He was sitting there and said, "Well, I better go." I said, "You want some coffeecake?" And I opened up the oven and pulled out the coffee cake.

He looked at me and said, "How in the world did you pack all of this stuff in by yourself?" I said, "There are two other guys with me." He said, "Oh. Well, where are they?" I said, "They're fishing in the raft." He said, "In the raft?"

He stayed with us for four days, and we were never going to tell him the truth. One day, while sitting in camp, he looked at the fuel bottles lined up on the shelf in the tree and he said, "What happened with those fuel bottles? They all have the same bend at the top. What happened to them?" Steve said, "Oh, we ran over them in the parking lot."

About two days later, R.J. was just outside camp using our alloyed hatchet to chop up branches. It didn't work very well. He stopped. He seemed to be analyzing the bend in the head of the hatchet, he then turned it on an angle and studied the angle. He turned around  and looked at the fuel bottles that were on the shelf in the camp kitchen. He looked at the hatchet then the fuel bottles a couple times, then he turned around and said, "Did you run over this at the same time as the bottles?" We just started laughing and at that point, we finally broke down and told him how we got everything there. I think we made front page of Bridgeport News. On the way out, we passed the Ranger who said, "Oh, you're coming from Benson. Were you there when the air drop happened?"

And we said, "No. What air drop?"

The next year, I started using the pack station to restock us at Benson. We planned an extended trip starting in Virginia Canyon. On that trip, we had Roger Kircher's mule "Blue" carry good food for the first week until the pack station restocked us at Benson. On the first day, we hiked up to Summit Lake where we met the Ranger Judy and invited her over for dinner. At dinner, we talked about the upcoming trip. After dinner, she said, "You know, it really struck me funny last year that you were the only group coming out of Benson who had no idea about the air drop."

We chuckled.

Then she said, "I can see that you're going to make a lot less of an impact this year than you did last year. The forest service sent someone in last year to retrieve the raft and oven you left for everyone to use."

BACK TO THE START AND INTO THE WORLD

When I was 4, almost 5, the world seemed to open up for me from that point on. I think it had to do with 3 important things that happened that year: moving into the new house (the Parkridge house), my silver piggy bank and our new dog Topper that we got for Christmas. All three of these seemed to launch me into a new world. They were very important in my life.

    I was born in 1948, and with the exception of the Viet Nam War, it's been a great time and generation to have grown up in. It was much different than today and somewhat innocent in comparison. There was a lot more trust and responsibility, accountability, respect, and freedom. We didn't lock our doors, and moms didn't worry about child predators. We left home to play outside and were not expected home until the street lights came on. There was common sense and a belief in God and country, manners, as well as a respect and politeness for the police and our elders when around them, despite all my tomfooleries.

The Parkridge House

I was born fourth-generation in Sacramento, California. My great-great-grandfather obtained a land grant from the Mexican government in Nevada City in 1846. The family had moved to Sacramento in the early 1900. We lived in a small house on Mead Avenue about mid-block in a new subdivision just south of William Land Park. It was a nice street and neighborhood where we knew many of our neighbors, primarily because of the other children on the block. It was a different time; not only did we know most of our neighbors we knew the milkman who delivered the milk to our doors and, in some cases, walked onto the back service porch and put the milk in the refrigerator while saying good morning to those gathered around the breakfast table. That was a common occurrence at our neighbors', the Giere's.

I was four when my dad built our new house, five houses down the street at the corner of Mead Avenue and Parkridge Road. It was a fantastic house and a home beyond its time. The ranch style home was "J" shaped with the long portion of the "J" on the Mead Ave. side, beginning at the top of the "J" with a large two-car garage with attached laundry and storage rooms then a 16-foot-wide covered breezeway that separated the house from the garage and was open to the raised red patio in the middle. Next was the formal dining room with windows overlooking the patio. Then a large "U" shape kitchen overlooked Mead Avenue, and in the corner was a large breakfast room. Across the bottom of the "J" along the Parkridge side was the breakfast room, the entry hall, guest bedroom and bath, the guest or boys' bathroom, and then the corner bedroom. Turning up the "J" was the 4th bedroom, then the master bedroom and bath. The middle of the "J" was a 30 x 30 raised red patio overlooked by the formal dining, living room, den and master bedroom windows. Many of the houses of the day had a living room and a family room. This house was different in that it had a very large living room and a small den.

The den was next to the living room, separated by a double-sided, floor-to-ceiling white quartz, rock fireplace. It was all paneled in cherry wood, so it was a fairly dark room and housed a very big roll-top desk Dad worked on. Later, it was also used as the TV room. We rarely used the front door facing Parkridge, but rather entered from the Mead Ave. side through a gate in a paneled wall that ran from the garage to the side kitchen door. Opening the gate leads through the breezeway to the raised red patio in the middle, or if you turn left, a 5' walkway leading to the side kitchen door was flanked by the painted paneled wall.

Beside being a fantastic house and floor plan, the cabinets in the kitchen and breakfast room along with the living room millwork and bookcase were of furniture-grade quality and lasted more than 60 years. There was a 1952 top-of-the-line stainless steel Hotpoint oven that did not work, but new owners could not find an oven to fit in the original hole and they didn't dare touch those cabinets because of the quality. But nothing lasts forever and the new owners have since remodeled it. The master bedroom had a 12-button light panel at the window overlooking the patio, breezeway and yard where all the exterior lights could be turned on or off. This was in 1952. Great house.

Lessons from the Silver Piggy Bank

That first Christmas in the new Parkridge house, my parents gave my brother and me these small silver piggy banks to put our money in. I believe it was one of the best things my parents did for me. They give us an allowance to cover the normal things they would buy and pay for anyway. My parents did not buy us things we wanted outside of buying us our clothes, Christmas presents or gifts for birthdays and holidays. They made us use our own money for what we wanted. Money was always part of the gifts at Christmas, birthdays and Easter. At Christmas and Easter, Mom and dad would hide coins in the fireplace rocks, all over the living room and in some of our presents. That money always went into the silver piggy bank. We received allowance and we could do extra work to make extra money, but they gave us the money to manage ourselves. There is a big difference between spending your own money as opposed to spending your parents' money.

When I was in the first grade, everyone was playing marbles and I wanted to buy a big bag of them for 89¢ at the five and dime store. But I did not have my money with me. My mom said she would loan me the money, and when we got home, I could pay her back, which I did. The next day, I took them to school and lost all of my marbles because I was not good at playing. That part did not bother me, but the fact that I lost 89¢ did.

It's an automatic teaching moment when you lose your own money because you made a mistake; nobody needs to tell you you've made a mistake. You feel it. Same thing happens in nature. She is a great teacher. You either go with her or you will pay the price and nobody has to tell you. Many times, I have been in the woods with kids and tell them they need to collect wood for their fire tonight knowing that they won't collect enough. Sure enough, they don't, so their fire goes out and they get cold. Same with "wash your oatmeal dish;" they don't and then have encrusted oat concrete on their dinner plate. I don't have to say a word. It's self teaching.

When I was in 3rd grade, Bank of America had a school savings program, and I got my first savings account with an envelope and a passbook for depositing money on a weekly basis. I liked making money and putting it into my savings account. I sold the Catholic Herald and peddled the Christmas cards around the neighborhood, and neighbors were familiar with me selling things. At Christmas, I went to the park, climbed the trees and collected the mistletoe, tied a red bow on it, put it in my wagon and sold it to the neighbors. I also went to the park and climbed the pine trees to the top and cut off a small Christmas tree that I would decorate and sell. It was a real money maker. Then I would put the money in the bank. The next year, two Christmas trees were growing at the top where I had cut one the year before. Dad talked a lot about making money, saving money, and setting goals for what you want. That sermon gave me guidance in my entrepreneurship. When I was selling my mistletoe, my dad said, "In selling, don't ask if they want one, ask how many do you want? More sales." When I would talk about something I wanted to do or make, he would say, "Don't talk about it, do it."

It seems things were handled differently then compared to how they are now. For example, around the block was my friend Russell Reid whose mother Marge had hired me to water the yard for the week when they went on vacation. I did a great job; every day I watered I had a Popsicle from their outside chest freezer. They arrived home and she was pleased with the job I did and paid me. About a week later, as I was playing with Russell, his mom offered us Popsicles. Well, when she went to get the Popsicle, she discovered that all but one were gone. Then I told her that was because I ate them while watering. She got mad at me, lectured me on stealing, and made me come back and do yard work to pay for the Popsicles I had eaten. That's the way things worked then. We were taught respect.

My friends and I wanted to build a soap box car made with a center board to sit on and two 2 x 4 cross boards for the axel and four wheels. We used a rope for our steering, so each of us put in a third of the money we thought we needed. We had already salvaged the wood from a construction junk pile but needed the axle, wheels, washers, cotter pins, U-nails center nut, bolt, and washers. The wheels were more expensive than we budgeted, so we were short of money to buy it all. They didn't have any more money and I did not want to ride back home and spend my money. We had gone to our neighbor Ralph Bilby's hardware store for our parts and pieces, and realizing we didn't have enough money for the steering nut bolt and washers, so we ended up stealing them! Four days later, an envelope from Bilby's hardware arrived in the mail addressed to me with a bill for the items we had stolen. Mom was so mad at me for stealing that she immediately made me go to my piggy bank and get the money to pay the bill, then took me down to the hardware store where I had to apologize in person to Mr. Bilby and pay for the stolen items. So, I ended up paying for it anyway.

This resulted in what I call, "Knock you down to build you up" moments with my dad, wherein he would chew me out to a point that I had to reach up to touch bottom. Who do you think you are?? Are you a thief?? Do you want to be known as a thief? Is that who you are? Is that the kind of person you are? A person who steals things? What were you thinking? You know better than that. After he had made his points, his berating would end abruptly, then he'd walk out to let me stew on what was said and my behavior. After some time, he would return and deliver another conversation to be more like a pep talk **"I knock you down to build you up."**

In this instance, he used it to enlighten and educate me on better ways of dealing with situations and made the point that I should have handled it the correct way and the way I was taught. That being, "Stand up and be forthright and honest."

I was taught that if I were forthright and honest, most people would work with you. In most cases, all you have to do is ASK. I should have explained to Mr. Bilby that though we needed the nut bolt and washers, we did not have enough money and could we pay him back later? Had I taken that approach, he may have just given us the parts or loaned us the money until paid back, which creates trust and accountability as opposed to being looked on as a bad kid and as a thief. Which way do you want to be viewed?

My Dog Topper

We had just moved down the street from our small house to the new Parkridge house. My mom and dad gave my brother and me a new dog for Christmas. As the story goes, it was a rainy day, and my dad was out looking for this pet for us. In the front window of the pet shop were all these brown and black dogs, and one white dog was over in the corner all by himself. So that's the one Dad brought home for us. He was a mix: half Spitz, half Cocker. He was just this little, white, fluffy ball when we first got him, barely big enough to get a tennis ball into his mouth; he was one of the greatest dogs that ever was.

He was a small dog, 38-40 lbs., pure white, with a little tan spot on his side and a little tan spot on his upright ears; we called him Topper. He had a stout little nose and sharp little teeth. He was mild-mannered at all times and smart as a whip, but he was also very aggressive when necessary. If my brother Bill and I got into an argument, he would come running into the room from wherever he was, stand between us and growl, looking at one then looking at the other. The first guy that moved towards the other got bit. At first, he was my brother's dog. Then when he got a little older, he became my dog, all the way up through my teenage years. Topper was my friend, my companion, my nurturer; he always had my back and was always with me until late in high school when he became my mom's dog.

In the early part of his life, the first year or two, he would take off and be gone for months at a time and then return. He did that three times until my mom had him neutered and then he stayed home. In those days, we didn't have all the dog laws of today; Topper never had a leash on him. He sat out on the Mead Avenue side of the yard and roamed the neighborhood. Everybody in the neighborhood knew who he was, and he was just a great dog. When I was in second grade, sometimes he would come over to Sutterville School at 2:30, just before the bell would ring for us to get out. He would come to the back door and just sit there until I was ready to end school.

As I said, Topper was a very mild mannered, well-behaved dog, friendly, until it was time not to be so. One day, he was about four or five houses down the block, almost at the Giere's, when I heard a ruckus. I could see two dogs fighting, one of them white, so I went running down there. Topper had gotten into a fight with a boxer, and I could see the boxer was on top of him, biting him. But then, as I approached, Topper got out from underneath the boxer and jumped up on top of his back. The fighting went on, back and forth.

I finally broke them up, and Topper was covered in spots of blood; I thought my dog was really hurt. The boxer started to run down the street back to wherever his house was. I had Topper in my arms and I got a hose to wash off all the blood and find out where he was hurt. I couldn't find any major cuts except for a gash on his nose, a cut on his forehead above the eye and a bite mark on his shoulder. After getting him cleaned up and on my way down to the Giere's house, I could see a trail of blood droplets on the sidewalk that disappeared into the street. That is because Topper with his sharp little teeth must have cut him deeply or hit a vein as there was a fair amount of blood. So, even though he was only 38 pounds, when it came time to be aggressive, he definitely could do that.

One time when I was about eight, I had gotten into an argument with a boy. I don't remember what it was about but I do remember being across the street with my dad and the other boy's dad. After a little discussion, we were instructed to shake hands and make up. Great, I put out my hand, and in his excitement the kid grabbed my hand and shook it up and down aggressively. Well Topper was about ten feet away with our two bicycles between us; he did not like the looks of the handshake and immediately ran, leaping over the bikes, and grabbed this kid, biting him in his side. Everyone knew it was caused by the aggressive handshake and it was a small bite, and in those days, we did not make a big deal out of things. Today, they would kill the dog and sue you. Mom did her best in helping me with baseball and batting practice; she would pitch to me and Topper would retrieve all the balls and bring them back to her.

Another time, Steve Crowle and I were fishing at the William Land Park duck pond. There was a group of boys, ranging from 5 to 18. There must have been six, maybe eight, of them. At any rate, we were getting along just fine and then all of a sudden, this one little kid slapped me in the face with a wet sock. "You don't do that!" I said. But he had the audacity to slap me again, I picked him up and threw him into the duck pond, which started the fight. Some of the bigger kids grabbed Steve and were beating up on him. Topper was up on the hill towards Fairytale Town, underneath a tree, trying to catch a squirrel, because he loved chasing squirrels. Steve let out a yell, "Topper!"

Topper came running off that hill and took a flying leap, turned sideways and grabbed the guy that was pounding Steve's head against the ground right in the side, just above his beltline, and drew blood. Then he turned and came after the guys that were in front of me, and bit a guy's calf as they ran away. Within 45 seconds, all of those people were gone.

Topper used to ride on my motor scooter; he'd sit on his haunches and lean back against me as we drove around. Sometimes we'd take him on our long bike rides around the Pocket Road and when he got tired, we'd just stick him up on my back, hang his front legs over my shoulders like a back pack, and he'd just ride that way all the way home.

They say you can't teach an old dog new tricks. One morning, when Topper was about 12, I wanted to teach him how to bring in the newspaper because the paperboy just put it on the front walk and didn't put it on the porch. I taught him how to pick up the newspaper. When he got the newspaper, he got a treat. After a couple mornings, I would let him out to get the newspaper, then I gave him a treat. One morning, he barked to go out again and I opened the door. A little bit of time passed and then he barked to come in. I opened the door and there were about five newspapers. He thought he was going to get a treat for each newspaper. I had to take them back.

Topper was really a smart dog, and I think a lot of it had to do with the fact that in the first year or two when he was out away from the house, he was really street smart. He never crossed the street without looking both ways. He had complete freedom to go anywhere he wanted to and he did, but he'd come back just in time to sit out on the Mead Avenue side lawn waiting for us to get out of school so he could go and do whatever we were doing.

We were up at the cabin one time, and I forget what my mom did to him, but it made him mad. He went and dug up one of the squirrels he had buried some time before and put it in her bed.

As the years went by, and I got older, Topper became my mom's dog. One time, my mom and dad had taken a trip into the foothills to Jackson. They stopped for gas, and somehow lost Topper, so they looked all over town. They stayed overnight. They checked the pound and they just couldn't find him anywhere. They decided to leave word and check with the pound up in the Jackson area later. So, they drove home late afternoon. When they got home, Topper was sitting on the Mead Avenue side lawn.

When I was 22, my mom called and said I needed to come get Topper and take him to the vet and have him put down because he couldn't hear and couldn't run, he couldn't see, and his teeth were falling out. Reluctantly, I said, "Okay, I guess it's time." He was almost 18. Mom said it was time. When I got there to pick him up, he was hiding. Supposedly, he couldn't hear me and he couldn't see me, but he knew where I was. He got out into the neighborhood and it took me about two hours to catch him. I took him home to my house, which was a strange home to him.

The vet said not to bring him in with the collar on, so I took his collar off of him. It was the first time in 17 years I ever took his collar off without putting him in the bath, and one of my daughters opened the door and Topper got out. We never saw him again. We tried everything, but without his collar and dog tags, we just could not find him.

MOM AND SELF-RELIANCE

My mom was my number one fan when it came to being creative and self-reliant. She always encouraged and allowed me to pursue whatever it was I was interested in doing. She exposed me to many things: travel, cooking, fine dining, to name a few. She had enough faith in me to allow me to make my first solo flight at five years old to Los Angeles to see my grandmother. When I returned and got off the plane, I did not acknowledge my parents because I was too cool and grown up in my blue shorts with suspenders, white shirt, and Bobby socks. Dad had business on Oahu and Kauai, and I made my first trip when I was 10 on the 4-engine, 9-hour, prop plane flight with big seats, great food, and service, but no movie. From ages 10 until 20, I made at least seven trips to the islands, traveling from the 4-engine prop plane into the jet age. When I was 12, we stayed at the Halekulani, for a month, which at the time was thatched-roof cottages. At that time, all that was on Waikiki Beach was the Moana Surfrider, the 2-story Outrigger Canoe Club, the Royal Hawaiian and then private homes all the way down to the Halekulani and Reef Hotel. We were there for a month and I had carte blanche approval to sign the bill to our room for whatever I wanted, whether it was to rent a surfboard, eat my cheese burger with a fried egg on it at the beach grill, or take an excursion. Mom always allowed me to be adventurous, so I signed up for a multi-island tour.

I was 12 and the wakeup call came for me at 4:30 in the morning. Mom said, "Why are you up this early?" I said, "I am going on a 4-island tour at 5:00 and will be back at 9:30 tonight."

"Oh ok," she responded.

It was a great day and tour. Me at 12 with a plane full of elderly grandparents.

Mom kept a clean house and expected us to do the same. If we did not put things away, she would hold any of our clothes or toys left on the floor in a lost and found box, then charge us a nickel to get it back. Through the years, every once in a while, she would find some incriminating evidence—dirty magazine, cigarettes, bobby pin or bowed barrette, etc. (tracks, as I call them)—then she would simply put it on my pillow to let me know that she knew and I was not getting away with it. "You can't kid an old kidder," she would say. I used this with my children also but changed the saying to "You're not blowing it by me." She didn't discipline directly but would let the issue rest for a day or two before her lecture and doling out her consequences. But if it were a major issue, she would pass it on to my dad. Most of the time, she addressed it directly and didn't tell dad.

She was big on saying I should listen to the angel on my shoulder. If you listen, you will get the right answers and maybe not do what you're thinking about doing. Moms know best, and it was about be here, be this way, act this way. One time, she told me not to take my money to the park. Turns out, some bigger kids beat us up and took the money. Another time, I put my baseball in the spokes of my bike and she said it was probably not a very good idea, that I might lose it. Guess what? I lost the ball. She was always reminding me to be good. She called me on my stuff and would let me know I wasn't getting away with it.

Dad would say, "Listen to your gut," but mom would say, "Listen to your guardian angel." Both can work, but you hear the angel first.

SERMONS FROM THE GREEN LEATHER CHAIR

What is important is the whole picture, whether I was standing at the corner of the coffee table receiving a statement or sitting at the end of the long couch. Dad's green leather chair was where my dad delivered his short statements, quips. and sermons, as I call them. It all started after we had moved into the new Parkridge house.

The sermons, as I call them, were continuous philosophical conversations that covered most areas of life: behavior, God, money, sports, business, politics, and local issues. He would often come at a particular subject from many different directions and different times to cement the point. Repetition was required for absorption and there was much to absorb. I didn't appreciate the full wisdom until many years of life had passed.

Quips were very important, one-liner life lessons that were delivered over and over in passing to remind me of the sermons that backed them up in great detail. These quips took residence in my brain and remain impactful on my life to this day. I use them all the time and have acquired some of my own.

My dad was a real estate man, through and through. He had no real hobbies except for work. He was not a sports guy, with the exception of being a fan of boxing and the New York Yankees. He often used sports as an example to get a point across or when trying to offer different approaches and examples to life. My relationship with my dad was a philosophical, business relationship. Similar to Harry Chapin's song "Cat's in the Cradle" (and the silver spoon): "I'm gonna be like you, Dad. You know I'm gonna be like you."

The living room of the Parkridge house was the stage upon which my life from 5 to 20 was played out. Almost everything taught and discussed was done in the living room from learning how to sell something, swing a golf club, field a ball, tie my tie, all the way up to and including how to dance and how to properly throw a punch.

I have included a picture of the living room showing the leather chair up against the white quartz rock fireplace. It wasn't so much that it was a big chair; it looked like a big chair because of the man sitting in it. To me, Dad was a towering figure of 6 feet who could be intimidating, especially if mad, not so much physically, but via facial and verbal tones. He commanded respect and had class most of the time. I did not sit in that chair too many times, a few when I was young, and it seemed like a very big chair to me. As a teenager, I remember sitting in his chair listening to Frank Sinatra (with a drink on the corner table to my right—just like dad).

Almost all his teachings, sermons, parables, life lessons, and quips occurred in the living room with him sitting in his green leather chair. From the beginning, the chair stayed there until my parents divorced. My dad's second wife still has the chair and it is shown on the cover of this book.

My mom (in the middle) was a 5' 2" blue-eyed, blond beauty who in those days was a homemaker who took care of the house and us kids. Dad was always busy, so my mom did her best to help me do the things I wanted to do. She encouraged my imagination, gave me freedom to explore, and bought me books on how things worked. I loved thumbing through the encyclopedias; it was my Internet for information. She did her best to cover the things Dad should have been doing. She was the one who took us to the mountains in the summer, played ball with me, taught me how to cook and paint, and walked me in to Desolation Valley on my first backpacking adventure. She also was big on manners and behavior, Emily Post, etiquette and the proper ways of conducting yourself.

The M-80

When I was about 9/10 years old, I was throwing my knife against the next-door neighbor's fence because it was a board fence. Our fence was a painted wall fence, and I didn't want to mess it up. I got into trouble with my neighbor for throwing my knife at their fence. Sometime later, I found my dad's stash of firecrackers that included a silver round cylinder with a green fuse; it was a little bigger than a firecracker, but it was a firecracker. I decided I was going to prank the next-door neighbor by dropping the firecracker in his indoor mailbox in the side light panel of his front door. I snuck up, lit it and dropped it into the mailbox, then ran down the front walk across the street. Before I could even jump in the bushes, I was expecting to hear a bang, instead I heard this huge "ka boom!"

    I turned around and saw the mailbox and side light window was gone. I don't know if the front door fell in on the floor or if it just blew open and stuck in the wall. But there was a six-foot hole in the front of this guy's house! He happened to be home sick with the flu and was sitting in his Barcalounger looking out through his front entry where there was no more door or sidelight panel. He got up from his recliner (I was hiding in the bushes across the street), walked out to the entry, checked out the damage, scratched his head and then disappeared to the back of the house. I figured he was going to call the cops.

I knew I was in big trouble and I did not want to get caught. I dashed out from the bushes, ran across the street and down a couple houses. I cut through their yard, up over the fence, through the rear neighbor's yard and out to Parkridge Road. I ran to the southwest corner of our house. I knew my dog Topper was going to be sitting by the side gate around the corner on the Mead Avenue side and would give me away, so I climbed over the side fence, ran down the side yard sprinted across the backyard and into the garage. I then climbed up to the 3' x 3' birdcage cupola on top of the garage and I had a 360-degree view of the whole neighborhood through the little three-inch round holes in this cupola.

After quite a while up in the cupola, I saw the cop car coming, and when something happens in the neighborhood, normally they go to the Giere's, the Grimes' or our house because of our older brothers. I could hear My mom talking to the police in the breezeway, saying, "He should be around here. I'm not sure." Then they came through the storage room into the garage, and were standing talking, directly below me. I was up in this cupola and my mom said, "Well, he can't be too far, because his bike's right here." Oh shit, I thought. Then she said, "But the dog's sitting out front, so maybe he went to the park." Then they walked out. I waited another 15-20 minutes up there, then I climbed down. I quickly snuck out of the garage through the storage room across the breezeway and up to the side kitchen door. My mom said, "Where have you been?" I said, "Oh, I went down to the park, why?" SAFE! I got away with it. They never found out who did it.

Some months later, on the 4th of July, my brother was using firecrackers to launch tin cans into the air when my dad came out with a coffee can and one of the M-80 firecrackers. He set it on a round metal lawn table and I wanted to tell him I didn't think that was such a good idea, but did not want to give myself away, so I said, "That looks a little bit big. Maybe we should stand back a little further." I thought it was going to turn that can into a grenade! Well, he lit it and when it went off, it blew the can sky high and crushed that metal lawn table like a beer can. My dad said, "Wow, I didn't think it was that powerful." I think he may have suspected I was the one who blew up the neighbor's front door after seeing it crush that steel table on the 4th of July and that's when this quip began.

"Do you know right from wrong?"

I didn't throw my knife against our painted wall because it would be wrong to damage it, but a board fence? What damage is a knife going to do to a board? I definitely knew I was wrong when the M-80 went off, and I knew immediately that I was in big trouble, but I got away with it.

Quip: Do you know right from wrong? Part one

Shortly thereafter my dad stopped me in the entry hall on his way out to work and said, "Hey, do you know right from wrong?" I said, "Yes." He said, "Well good, because I can't be with you."

Then he would walk away. Happened all the time through the years!

"Do you know right from wrong" was a constant reminder to make me think about what I might be doing. It started some time after the M-80 incident. Because of the sermons, I already knew right from wrong.

JACK

In the neighborhood, the Gieres' house was like a second home to me, as Jack was my childhood and lifetime friend. We pulled many shenanigans and had great parties. As kids, we did all kinds of stuff just for fun, like farting into the new tape recorder, making prank calls, listening to party lines, and shooting out the Christmas tree lights with our B.B. guns on those foggy nights. I remember all of us children lining up in the Gieres' entry hallway to get our polio shots from Dr. Giere. We sold Christmas cards to earn points to trade in for items in Christmas card catalog. I bought a pup tent with my points and Jack traded his for a bugle because he is a music man from a musical family. In high school, he was in a band called the Marauders and opened for the Beach Boys several times at the Memorial Auditorium. In fact, the Beach Boys later recorded Jack's song Barbara Ann as their own hit.

We did some foolish and crazy things, like one time, we found a box of 22 bullets and were hitting them at the tail end with a hammer. After whacking about five shells, I said, "Jack, I don't think this is such a good idea. We do not know where these bullets are going. Jack said, "You're right and we stopped. When we were about fourteen, Jack bought an old 1941 black ford for $175. With a down payment of $18 and a note for the rest, he parked the car down the street around the corner on Park Mead. That way, he could drive out of the neighborhood without getting caught by our mothers. We had a lot of fun in that old jalopy. Jack never did get caught driving, but being 15 and not knowing that you need to check the oil. while driving home he blew an engine rod coasted to a parking lot and then walked home. I don't know if he ever paid off the car balance.

One particular antic sticks out in my mind. It was 1965, early in our junior year, when Jack had gotten a joint from some other guys he knew. We decided we would take it into the far corner of his backyard. We started smoking it and after a bit, we expected a helicopter to fly in and bust us; we didn't know much about it. After smoking a little bit more, Jack took off for the house and up the stairs he went. I was not sure what he was doing but I was right behind him as he went up the stairs and burst through his parents' door. He jumped on his parents' bed screaming, "I am going to die—I am going to die—I just smoked marijuana. Slowly and quietly, I turned and walked out of the house and back home, puzzled as to what just happened. I thought, "Tomorrow will be a better day." That belief has done more for me in my life than any other.

In high school, we were both in "36," a high school fraternity started originally as a "book club" in the early 1900s. We had a great time organizing and running community work parties and dances. Most Friday nights, we would get a keg of beer then drive up the Jackson highway to the caves just short of the town of Ione. We had many drunk and wild nights. But we were away from trouble.

Jack and I ordered a pizza and pitcher of beer and got arrested the night before our graduation for fake IDs. Then a couple years later, we went to Oregon to Lane Community College trying to get into the university. We had rented a house that was just off campus and because of Jack's electric piano, we made friends with Quincy Brown and the guys from the Sigma Ki house. We had many good parties and only got busted once by the police. But when you party too much, your grades show it and we were only there a year and then uncle Sam came calling.

Jack has continued in a legacy of his mother's Christmas parties whereby many of our high school friends and fraternity brothers still gather to party and sing with our piano man Jack until 3:00 in the morning. He has kept us together for 50 years plus. Priceless.

My Friend Chris King

Chris King and I have been best of friends, close friends, for the last 60+ years. I met Chris when we were 10. I probably didn't meet him before that because our blocks were separated by a horse pasture that is now Sherwood Ave., and we went to different schools. On his block, he had a whole bunch of kids that he played football with, and on my block, I had a whole bunch of kids that I played football with. So, Chris and I decided we would have a block against block game. We organized a game and we had an older boy referee; I think his name was Corky French. We played the quarters out by the number of plays, and we fielded each side with seven or eight kids. It was a great game.

It was a seesaw game all the way through. Chris's team drove towards the goal as the last-quarter plays were winding down. He drove to our 15-yard line and on the last play of the game, he kicked a field goal and won the game. We have been friends ever since and they just don't make them any better than my friend Chris. I am so fortunate to have such a friend. We are like an old married couple where either one of us can look at the other and know exactly what he is thinking. And we have never had a fight, he might walk away just shaking his head, but we don't need to fight about it. I could write another book about the trips, adventures and shenanigans Chris and I experienced together, some of which will be revealed later. We worked together for 25 years and have hunted ducks together every year since high school. Extremely special.

Rats for Mrs. Vest

At some point during elementary school, a friend from down the street Greg Merrett had a basement and he also had a couple of domestic rats, which he kept in a wooden crate box. Quickly, the two little rats were four little rats, then eight rats, then 16 rats. He kept adding boxes and boxes and the 16 turned into 32, the 32 into 64, then his mom said he had to do something with all the rats.

He was trying to figure out what he was going to do with them, so Greg decided we were going to put them in a box and prop them up against Mrs. Vest's front door. She was the principal of Sutterville School and lived around the block on Francis Court. We took the box over there and set it up so when the door opened, the box would fall over. We rang the doorbell. Mrs. Vest opened the door, the box fell over, and 60 or 70 rats went all through the house.

Some 30 years later, at Jack Giere's Christmas party on Mead Avenue, I told her it was Greg and me. Even after 30 years, boy was she was still pissed. There were many times I ignored "right from wrong" and told Mom's guardian angel to shut up.

Kool-Aid Stand

Because of the silver piggy bank, I always liked having my own money, and in the hot Sacramento summer when I was 10, I wanted to make money. I thought, "Well, I am going to run a Kool-Aid stand." But Kool-Aid stands never really make a lot of money because there aren't enough customers. I had heard Dad's business stories and points, so I knew to be successful that "location-location-location" was very important. And I also knew it was important to "not talk about it, but do it." We lived down the street from William Land Park, which has a golf course. I was always over in the park, and I knew it well. On the golf course, hole 7 is a quick par 3, whereas the 8th hole is a long par 5.

The tee for the 8th hole was under this very big oak tree, which provided great shade. I figured I had a captive foursome that had to stand around for four or five minutes before they could tee off; I had customers all day long. I borrowed $5 from Mom and bought Kool-Aid, sugar and cups. I spent about $3.80, made my Kool-Aid and went to the 8th hole. That first day, I made almost $10, paid Mom back her $5 and went out and bought my needed Kool-Aid supplies again.

I'd make the Kool-Aid the night before and put it in two Coleman containers with big lids in Mom's large chest freezer. In the morning, it had about four inches of slush on top, then I got a nickel more for the slush. I also figured out that if I put free ice cubes from Mom's freezer in the cups, I could increase the cup sizes, charge a nickel more and not use any more Kool-Aid product.

    I was doing really well. Every day, I got a little bit bigger until finally I had a big cardboard box for a counter, three wagons and a place for people to put the cups in the trash. Then I started serving iced tea and lemon wedges along with the Kool-Aid. The clubhouse got a little ticked off at me because I wasn't just the little kid selling Kool-Aid; I was competition. They sent the cops who evicted me from the golf course. At the time, the golfers were saying to the police, "You have got to be kidding me." Two days later, I went back and tried it again and the cops came out and removed me from the golf course again. So, that was the end of my Kool-Aid stand. But I had a good two-week run and put over a $150 in my savings account. To put this into perspective, $10.00 would have bought a family of four a week's worth of food.

My Bank

When I was 8, I had a savings account at the Wentworth branch of Bank of America. At home, I would empty my silver piggy bank into a metal strong box that Mom had bought me as a birthday present. It was the size of a large shoe box and had a combination lock on it for safe keeping until I deposited it into my savings account so I always had some money on hand. This metal box was my private lockable storage box that only I had the combination to. Besides keeping my cash locked and safe, I used it through the years to store and hide all those things you hide from your mom. Knives, dirty magazines, fire crackers, cigarettes then later condoms and pot. It is funny that I know my mom and her house helper Mildred tried many times to get into that box. One time, they actually bent the lid with a screwdriver trying to get into it, but were unsuccessful.

In some of the business sermons, there was information on money, the power of money, borrowing and loans and the responsibilities associated with them. It was the sermon of how banks make money and the benefits or pitfalls of leveraging and borrowing.

I was around 11 when my brother borrowed $20. In my loan docs, as you might call it, or my lending paper, my IOU, my interest rate was usurious, and the penalties were just outrageous. If he didn't pay on time, they added up really quickly. So, my brother didn't pay on time, and after a while, the penalties were adding up to such a huge amount, I said, "Hey, you need to pay the bill. You don't owe me $20, you owe me $40 now because of all the penalties and interest."

He objected, so we took it to my dad, sitting in his big, green chair. And my brother said, "This is not fair and I shouldn't have to pay this."

I said, "Well, he should have to pay because he agreed to pay."

My dad said, "Well, the penalty is a little bit high."

I said, "Here's the loan agreement. He signed it."

My dad read it and looked at my older brother, who is five years older than me, and said, "You did sign this."

So, we settled it by cutting the penalties out and he had to pay the current interest rate plus principle.

Yes, I had a little bank in the house. And if you needed money, I could loan it to you.

Quip: Never Be Classed

My dad often said, "Never be classed, don't be a rich kid, don't be a poor boy, don't be a bully, and don't be a sissy, make everyone your friend."

Tough order, but I liked it.

Never be classed was a big one for me, as it was a sermon based on being a good person, a good citizen, a hard worker, a leader, accepting and humble. I believe this quip came up just before or just after I started the fourth grade at St. Robert School, a new Catholic school located in a working-class neighborhood and district where the kids did not have the gifts I had. I was well aware of my dad's success because of the Parkridge house, the Cadillac cars they drove, and all that came with it in comparison to others. As a kid, I did not want to be classed as a rich kid, so this quip meant a lot to me because there is a lot to it. "Never be classed" means don't be classed in a negative way, but it's ok to be classed in a positive way.

In addition to that, it was about life, people and acceptance. "Make everyone your friend" was part of the quip that helped me develop my accepting attitude towards people. But by the time I got to high school, the stigma of the rich kid seemed to disappear.

Saint Robert School

In kindergarten and first grade, I went to Holy Spirit School, but then I went to Sutterville Elementary for second and third grades. I don't know why but I think it was because my brother wanted to transfer to Sacred Heart School and Holy Spirit said to take both of us out. So, I guess you could say I got kicked out of Holy Spirit in the first grade. At any rate, there was a new parish being formed and we started attending mass in an old ranch-style strip center that is now Raley's supermarket. Saint Robert School was being built and my mom wanted me to go there, so we started going to church at saint Roberts. My mom was able to get me registered even though I was not in their district. Because it was a brand-new school, our class was the first graduating class starting in the fourth grade. So, we were always the top class. What a class it was, a real cast of characters and talented people.

Sister Mary Antonio was the only nun who could handle us. One time, I think it was fifth grade, we were studying religion and I raised my hand and said, "Yesterday, you said God knows all, sees all, and is everywhere."

Sister Antonio replied, "Yes."

"So, He knows what you did yesterday and what you're doing today and tomorrow."

Sister again replied, "Yes."

Then I said, "So He already knows whether you're going to heaven or hell, so what difference does it make?"

The whole class thought I had a point. Sister Antonio tried the rest of the day to convince us that we were not predestined, but we did not buy it. So, she brought in Father McTag the next day and then the monsignor on the third day before we were convinced that it is determined by your own choices and you are not predestined.

One Friday in 5th grade, I got my sack lunch that mom had made for me and discovered that she had made a baloney sandwich on a no meat Friday. I realized she just made a mistake, no big deal. But then some kids saw the Bologna and said, "You can't eat meat on Fridays, it's a mortal sin and you're going to hell." I looked up at them while sitting and said, "Really? Tell you what, you find in the Bible where it says you can't eat meat on Friday." I knew this because of conversation I had had with Dad when, as part of an example of a marketing tool or strategy, he explained that the pope of the past had made that rule to support the fisherman and that is why we eat fish on Fridays.

When I was in the 6th grade, I flew to Los Angeles to visit with my grandmother. One night, she was going out with her friend Gladys and was going to take me to some girl's birthday party that I did not want to go to. I didn't know anybody and thought it was a terrible idea, but I had to go anyway. Once there, the party started and I quickly became aware that southern California kids were far ahead of us here in Sacramento, the small, hick farm town, Sacratomato.

Everyone got into a circle and the birthday girl stepped to the center put down a bottle and spun it. When it stopped spinning, it was pointed right at me! So she came over and planted a long kiss on me that started the night. Boy did I have a good time. When I got home, I told everyone about it and said we have to have some spin the bottle parties. Well, we got away with 3 or 4 until the nuns found out and put an end to the parties.

In 7th grade, my friend Steve Crowle and I decided to cut school the day before Easter vacation, thinking they would not miss us and forget by the time vacation was over. Our mistake was telling some of our classmates what we were going to do because four other boys showed up at the Raley's parking lot the next morning to cut school with us. It was not hard for the school to figure it out when six boys from the same class were absent. We had a great day riding our bikes around Pocket Road only to arrive at home with all of our parents waiting for us.

We had the ugliest uniforms: turquoise shirts with a maroon S-R-S embroidered on the pocket and brown corduroy pants. The girls had turquoise blouses and maroon polyester jumpers and skirts. This was ok until the latter part of sixth grade and into seventh grade when I started my own rebellion trying to get the school to change the uniform. Periodically, I would not wear my uniform and Sister would say, "Tom, where is your uniform?" and I would say, "Hanging in my closet."

Sister replied, "Why didn't you wear it?"

"I might say, 'It's ugly' or 'We look like spring flowers' or 'I was walking by Joaquin Miller School.' And it's embarrassing."

I even had a white shirt embroidered with S-R-S but that didn't work. The rest of the class never got behind my idea. I left and went to Joaquin Miller School in the 8th grade because of the uniform.

Some 50 years later, I attended the funeral of a friend at the new Saint Robert Church. During the ceremony, I was looking at the new church and new alter and tabernacle then I noticed the old smaller tabernacle over on the sidewall in a small alcove. My memory then flashed back to my parents talking in the breakfast room about donating the tabernacle to the church. I didn't think much of the conversation at the time because I was a kid, but I had to chuckle when it dawned on me that is how my mom got me into Saint Robert.

QUIP: YOU WOULDN'T CARE SO MUCH WHAT PEOPLE THOUGHT OF YOU IF YOU KNEW HOW LITTLE THEY DID — DON'T WORRY ABOUT IT.

Don't get yourself all bent sideways based on your unknown perception that things and thoughts of other people are about you. It ties back into my own quip of "it's not on their plate." If it is on your plate, take care of it quietly and don't stir the pot. Nobody cares what's on your plate or in your glass. They may be sympathetic, but it's not on their plate.

Gold Doorknob Theory

In October, Dad was a big New York Yankees fan and often went to New York for the World Series. While there, Mom would visit FAO Schwartz to buy Christmas presents. Because we had our own money, she did not buy us things, but at Christmas, she sometimes went overboard and gave too many presents. I put many of the presents in my closet before any friends came over so they would not see all the gifts I had gotten. I left out just enough to show what I got for Christmas.

One year, she bought me a really neat mountain train tunnel with its own waterfall; it was expensive! I told mom I appreciated the gift but it was too expensive and I would rather make and decorate my own mountain tunnel out of paper mache. So, she returned it and gave me money for my tunnel project.

There was a point when my friends started razzing and teasing me about the gold doorknobs on my house. They kept it up for a while and it really bothered me, so I told my dad about it. He said, "You tell them the doorknobs are not gold; they are made of brass just like everyone else's knobs are. They are just a heavier grade. You tell them they're not your doorknobs, they're your dad's and if you want doorknobs like these then you will have to work and buy them yourself." The next time the razzing happened, I got mad and told them what my dad said. That ended the razzing.

Shortly after this incident, Dad delivered a sermon on what it takes to have a house like the Parkridge house. If you want these things, then you must WORK, WORK, WORK. Even if you don't feel good, you work and push through it. You cannot accomplish it without WORK.

Quip: WORK, WORK, WORK

I grew up in privilege. I was aware of where I came from and where others came from. Mom and her teachings included Emily Post, the proper way of doing things and the proper way of acting. They would take me to San Francisco and asked if I wanted room service and to watch TV. I would always say no I want to go with you to experience good gourmet foods; I had escargot the first time when I was 7. Dad made it very clear that I lived in his house and if I wanted the same things later then I would have to work, work, work for them. I knew this, but none of my friends or classmates knew. They could see I came from a rich household, and I was fearful that because of it, I would be classed as a rich kid.

The sermons like this one encompassed many of the other teachings and quips that run together; they were just expressed in different ways. Included in this one could have been "take care of yourself," be tough. If you get knocked down, get up and try again. You are responsible for you. Save your money; when you're 18, you are on your own. Be prepared.

All dad knew was work. He didn't have the experience of all the other interests and hobbies I have, with the exception of duck hunting. My dad, although not an avid hunter, at the time was invited to join the Sacramento Outing a premiere duck club in the Butte Sink. It gave us a father-son bonding adventure time together from age 10 to 20. It's also the reason I have hunted ducks ever since.

We didn't take a lot of family vacations except for a few and then many of those trips were tied to business in Hawaii. Most of our summers were spent at the cabin in the mountains with Mom. In 1955, when I was 8, Dad took us to Disneyland and did it first-class, as we arrived in a helicopter. There were other short trips to San Francisco and Carmel, gourmet dining, tuna fishing and vacation on Balboa Island. In 1963, he took me to New York for the Giants-Yankee World Series. Dad had to buy scalped tickets for the last game. I sat by myself in Yankee Stadium directly behind home plate about 10 rows up where I watched Tom Haller, catcher for the Giants, hit a grand slam homerun in the 9th inning to win the game and send it back to San Francisco where the Yankees finally won the series. What a memorable day.

While there, I wanted to go to Abercrombie and Fitch. We were staying at the St. Regis just off Fifth Ave. I grabbed a cab not knowing the store was three and a half blocks away. Getting into the cab was 10 cents when the flag went down and another 15 cents to the store; I gave the cabby 50 cents. He turned to me and said "Hey kid, I don't know where you're from." "I am from California." "But here in New York, we believe in tipping." Well in my mind, a 15-cent tip on a 35-cent fare was a good tip, so I said, "Oh I am sorry, give me back that money," while pulling out a bill. He handed the 50 cents to me, and I gave him back the 35 cents and got out of the cab.

While on the New York trip, we were all in the hotel bar getting ready to go out to dinner one night. Dad and his friends Everett and Charlie ordered a drink, and when the bartender asked me what I wanted, I said, "I will have a Jack Daniels over." He said, "You must have a tie on." Dad said, "Go get your tie." I was 15 and the drink was waiting for me when I got back.

The Empire State Building, Sugar Ray's Bar in Harlem, three games at Yankee Stadium, New York restaurants. One night, we went to a gourmet diner in Connecticut in a country-style house. I think it was named Christina's where I had had the most memorable dish called Boola, Boola. It was served in a copper bowl with a candle under it to keep it hot. It was turtle and potato soup. So good that I still remember it today; it was a two-week trip and a great experience, education.

SOS

I learned Morse code in school and learned that SOS was dot, dot, dot, dash, dash, dash, dot, dot, and dot. I told this to my friend Jack and we wanted to see if it really worked. Our house was not too far from the Executive Airport, so we got up on our roof with a flashlight and whenever a plane came by, I would flash them "dot, dot, dot, dash, dash, dash, dot, dot, dot." We did that for about 45 minutes or so. Then, out of the east, I could see the lights of another plane that was coming straight at us and coming closer. I started signaling again, "dot, dot, dot, dash, dash, dash, dot, dot, and dot." It got closer and closer. "Dot, dot, dot, dash, dash, dash, dot, dot, dot."

All of a sudden, two huge floodlights came on and lit up the whole house. We ran across the living room roof and ducked behind the fireplace chimney and hid as they came over the top. Then as the helicopter made the turn to check again Jack and I ran across the breeze way roof and hid behind the bird cage cuppola on the top of the garage as they made the second pass. Now, today they'd arrest you, but they probably just said, "Ah, it's just a kids doing SOS." The point is that if you ever get lost, you can signal. You can signal with a mirror. You can signal with a flashlight. It's very easy to get somebody's attention by signaling.

Through the years, I told my friend Chris King that I could signal him across Lake Tahoe; he had a cabin at Al Tahoe and we had a family cabin at Emerald Bay, which is about eight miles away. I took a three-inch compact mirror and could hit a target if I stuck my arm out like a gun barrel and sighted it through the "V" in my fingers then flicked the mirror so it reflected on my fingers. I kept telling him I could do it. One morning, I got up and took my wife's 3" compact mirror and started signaling because I knew he'd be out on his deck having coffee. A minute later, my phone rang. He said, "Is that you?" I said, "Yeah. It's me." Then he asked, "How big is that mirror?" I said, "It's three inches." He said it looked like it was 5 feet by 5 feet.

Some years later, I was telling the same story to Mike Carrigan on our way out from Benson Lake when we were camped in Kerrick Meadows. It was dark with no moon and I noticed there was a jet airliner coming across the sky, way out there to the right at, say, 35,000 feet. I said to Mike, "Watch this." I took my flashlight, pointed it at him and held it on, then I turned the light off. I did it again, turned it on, held it on him, and turned it off. Turned it back on, held it on him, and turned it off again. And on the fourth time I did it, the pilot turned off his lights and Mike said, "Oh man, did you see that? He turned off his lights."

Now, if you think about it, the lights that are on the airplane when he is flying by, that you see, those are small, little lights on the end of the wing. They're not very big. And if you can see their light, they can see your light, especially if you're the only light in a huge area that has no lights. The pilot just let me know he could see my light. So, if you ever get lost, SOS.

QUIP: LISTEN, LISTEN: LISTEN TO THE OTHER GUY AND YOU WILL KNOW WHAT HE KNOWS AND WHAT YOU KNOW.

This one can be used every day. One of the lead-ins Dad used for this quip was fishing because we were at the cabin and I wasn't catching as many fish as others were. But he also repeated it many times over the years using different examples. He'd say, "Ask the guy who is catching the fish what he's using, what he is doing, what his secrets are." Educate yourself by asking and listening. Little did I know how important it was that I listen to my dad, his sermons and his life lesson quips.

Judo Lessons

As I mentioned, many activities took place in the living room, whether it was to learn how to dance, swing a bat, or field a ball. Dad had already taught me how to properly throw a punch (in the living room) and always told me "Even though you may be small, do not let anyone push you around—and know how to defend yourself if needed—you don't have to fight to stand up for yourself. When I was about 10 or 11, we had a Japanese exchange student Kogi who lived with us. He had been taking me to judo lessons. One night, I came home still in my gi, my judo clothes, one night after judo class and my dad, sitting in his green leather chair asked me how judo was. I said it was fine.

He said, "What did you learn?"

I said, "How to flip someone. I can flip you."

"No, you can't."

"Yes, I can. Come here and I will show you."

He got up from his chair and came over to me. I said, "Bend over so I can grab ahold of the lapel of the jacket or in your case the tie with my right hand and then your sleeve at the elbow with my left hand."

After I was set and had a hold of him, I quickly turned 180 degrees swinging my right elbow up under his arm pit while holding on to his tie and at the same time pulling on his sleeve and bending over. I laid him out flat on the living room floor with a thud! Oh, was he pissed!

Because of the loud thump noise, my mom came running out of the kitchen only to see Dad pissed off and picking himself off the floor and me standing over him. She wanted to ask what happened but couldn't because Dad was yelling at me.

"Calm down, calm down, Bill," she said, "What happened?"

He stopped yelling at me and I took that moment to say, "I am sorry but it is not fair that you are mad at me when I told you what I could do and then proved it. Not fair and you're not hurt, are you?"

With that, he smiled, started to laugh, and said, "You're right, I'm sorry."

QUIP: DON'T TALK ABOUT IT – DO IT

Dad quoted this one and "listen to the other guy" many times and was backed up by the sermon on planning, doing and accomplishing what it is that you want. If you want something, figure out what is needed to accomplish and go after it.

This one encompasses the sermon relating to being competitive, winning, and working smart and hard. It was about not bragging or exaggerating what you're doing or flaunting your success. Don't talk about it; they can see it! So you don't need to tell them. Be humble.

There were times I used his teaching to get what I wanted from him. Like the Pool Decision

Dad always taught me to stand up for what I believed and I did so with him many times. I heard my parents once again talking about putting a pool in the backyard, as they had been for some time. So, I walked into the living room, stood at the corner of the coffee table in front of my dad sitting in his green leather chair and said, "You need to build the pool while we're still young enough to enjoy it. So don't talk about it; do it." Then I walked out, just like Dad always did. A short time later, we were laying out the shape of the pool with a garden hose and the pool was built.

The Skateboard Dummy

On Mead Avenue, the cars used to just roar down the street because it was about a straight half a mile. The parents always complained. We were always playing tricks on cars. We would stretch a string across the street at bumper height and you tie cans at the ends. When the cars drive by, they pick up the string and then they drag these cans behind the car all the way down the road. We'd throw water balloons and oranges at them, and all that kind of stuff.

One time, we made a stand-up skateboard dummy. We got on the other side of the road with a string and we would pull the dummy across the road on the skateboard in front of cars that were speeding. We'd watch them just slam on their brakes, go sideways, and be all freaked out. But one time, we did it to this one guy and he couldn't stop and ran right over the dummy. The driver just smacked it. He stopped the car and he got out, probably thinking he'd killed this guy, right? Then he found out that it was a dummy. Oh, let me tell you, was he pissed. He was looking all over for us, but he never did find us. It was the last time we did that one because somehow Dad found out about it. Turns out he knew the man driving the car, which then resulted in another "knock you down to build you up" moment with my dad.

Quip: Do you know right from wrong? Part 2: The Risk Area

On many occasions, as I got older, my father would stop me in passing and say, "Do you know right from wrong?" "Yes." "Well, good, because I can't be with you." Then he would start to walk away as he had in the past, but now, after hesitating for a second, he turned back to me and said, "You know, there is a grey area between the two and that is called the risk area. I want you to always consider the risk because if you take the risk and you get caught, you will pay the consequences and I will not bail you out. Am I clear?" "Yes," I answered.

Do You Want to Buy Some Stock?

I was 12 years old and my dad said, "How much money do you have saved?"

I said, "$850."

He said, "Whoa. That is pretty good. Where did you get that money?"

"I got that money from my Kool-Aid stand and my mistletoe sales, saving my allowance, birthdays and Christmas and all that kind of stuff."

Then he said, "Do you want to buy some stock?"

I said I didn't know. "What is it?"

He said, "Well, we're going to buy Sacramento Savings. Hopefully, we will do well and if you buy some stock, you might make some money."

I said, "Do I have to spend all my $850?"

He said, "Yes."

"I think I will have to think about that."

"I understand, but think about this. You have $850. I will match your $850 and you can buy $1,700 worth of stock and when you sell it, you pay me back the $850, no interest." I said, "You got a deal." Just after turning 16, we sold the stock for $3,850. I paid my dad back the $850 that I owed him. Then I ordered and paid for my new 1965 GTO.

Fast Cars, Muscle Cars

My brother had a 1957 black Chevy with a 283 engine that was very fast. Muscle cars were the big thing at the time, and I wanted the fastest car I could buy. The Ford Mustang had just come out, and Dad thought that was the car I should buy, but I wanted a GTO. I searched for the best deal and ordered and paid cash for my brand new 1965 GTO. It took three months for delivery. It was maroon with black interior: 389 cubic inches of raw power with three two-barrel carburetors a 390-rear end and four on the floor with an 8-track tape player. It was a real beauty. I ordered it from Olsen Pontiac in Marysville.

Chris and I drove my Corvair to pick up my new car. Chris played with me to race all the way home but I wanted to break it in slowly. I did not go over 50 miles an hour or rev the engine over 3000 rpm for the first 500 miles, and I changed the oil at 250. By doing this, I believe it resulted in a perfectly balanced engine and the fastest car in Sacramento. We'd hang out at TottMan and Ripley's Flying "A" filling station at the corner of Sutterville and South Land Park. It was a time when American Graffiti was fading, but cruising downtown K Street was still the thing to do.

We picked up a lot of drag races and only raced for money, $50 minimum. I never got beat with the exception of one night. I raced Aubree Pritchard who had a brand new 396 Chevelle, I fell asleep at the starting flag and he hole shot me. I just could not make up the difference to beat him. Later, we went to Sacramento Raceway for a grudge race and

I beat him handily. Another time, we picked a race with these guys from Stockton driving a Chevy Malibu with 283 stickers on the side. I barely beat him and when Chris went to collect the money, the guy said he had never been beaten before and that was because he was running a 425 Corvette engine under the hood.

Another time, after winning by three car lengths, Chris went to collect and the guy said, "Boy that car is fast. He should go race a guy by the name of Tom Cook." Chris said, "You just raced him!" It was a great car and we had many good times in it. We made a lot of money with that car, but it got stolen. The thieves took the batteries and American mags and burned it. Years Later, the word on the street was it was stolen by two brotherz that went to McClatchy. I won't mention the namez.

In hindsight, I think it would have been a better choice to buy a VW bus and invest the remaining money into something else. I think we would have had more fun in the bus than in the GTO. On Friday nights, everyone would go cruising downtown on K street. For some reason, we did not do well with the girls in the GTO, we did better in my Corvair. Maybe too much of a rich kid car? But we had no problem picking up a drag race and made money doing it. Knowing I could never replace it, I bought an MGB sports car.

Early Primitive Inklings

Most summers, we spent time at the Sayles Canyon cabin just above Camp Sacramento. What was great about the cabin was summer in the Sierras, and we had complete freedom to hike, fish, and explore, just being in nature. It was lots of fun to go to Camp Sacramento. Nickel ice cream cones, talent show and Saturday night dances. Looking back, what I enjoyed most was the atmosphere was more family-oriented. We ate together, did dishes by hand together, and played board games. This did not happen at home. I loved to get up early in the morning on Sundays and fire up the woodstove to make dollar pancakes from scratch as my grandmother's helper Annie taught me. Sift dry ingredients and fold in the egg whites...delicious.

Dad would come up for the weekends. Mom took care of us and was such a good sport; she would help clean the fish and do our laundry. In the beginning, she used an old ringer washing machine that was in the woodshed along with the old icebox and double cast iron laundry sink, which I took a bath in as a little kid. I spent every summer up there from the time I could crawl.

Mom would take us to the cabin every summer. Primarily, we fished, but we also explored, built log and stick forts (shelter) and slept out in them.

Dad always told stories about riding his horse from Sacramento to the cabin, about climbing Horsetail Falls and going into Desolation Valley beyond.

It is one of the reasons I went backpacking at 12.

Quip: Class is hard to describe, but you know it when you see it.

This sermon was again about life and your attitude towards it and yourself. How you handle your success, behavior, and money. How you carry yourself, how you treat other people, and your self esteem. Dress properly. Be humble and giving. Be a person with outstanding character. Everyone knows a person who has class because you can see it. Is it standing in the mirror? This applies to everyone from the bus boy to the CEOs. You do not have to have a lot of money to have class. This also tied back into never be classed, negatively.

QUIP: I NEVER MET A MAN I DIDN'T LIKE, IF I TOOK THE TIME TO KNOW HIM. BUT I HAD A CHOICE OF WHO I TOOK THE TIME WITH.

This quip was about not being judgmental and being open and accepting and friendly; being trusting until proved otherwise. But you have the choice of who you take the time to know, and it does not take long to figure that out.

My dad spoke many times in parables and examples. This one started at a young age to teach acceptance of people and probably needs more explaining. It actually goes along with a story he told about a man he passed every morning in the alley on his way to the office. Every morning, he would say, "Good morning" to the man and would get nothing back but a grumble. His thought was "What an ass." But as time went by, he had the opportunity to get to know him and discovered he wasn't an ass; that's just the way he was in the morning. Some people are grumps in the morning or have work on their mind; it does not mean they're a bad person. That's just the way they are. Be accepting.

School Change

Because I disliked the St. Robert's uniforms and the turquoise shirts, I decided I wanted to go to Joaquin Miller, Jr. High School in 8th grade. This public school had classes that were not available at St. Robert. They had classes for home economics, wood shop, metal shop and the President Kennedy physical fitness program that was self motivating. We could earn different symbols of achievement on our gym shirt all the way to the five gold Olympic rings. It was a great gym program. I elected to take metal shop; it was one of the best classes I ever took and was taught by an incredible teacher by the name of Bernie Jorgensen.

    We learned so much in his class and had fun doing it. At the time, little motor scooters and tote goats were the things to build. This is a couple years before the Honda 50 showed up. I had bought a frame for $10 that had bicycle front forks, wheels and a rear sprocket but no engine. I went to the junk yard and bought several incomplete engines for the parts and worked on getting it running. After tinkering with all the parts and pieces, trial and error, I finally got it running. What an education. I mounted it to the frame, bought the centrifugal clutch and chain and I had a motor scooter. The engine didn't have much power and I wanted a better engine. While riding to my friend's house on the next block over, I passed by a house who's garage door was open and I saw a lawn mower with a really nice engine on it.

That night I snuck over there with my wagon, tools and crescent wrenches. The garage door was still open, so I walked in, removed four bolts and stole the engine. I took it home, cleaned and painted it then mounted it on my scooter. It was a bigger and better engine and I could go much faster on this rickety frame with bicycle front forks that was not built for that use. This had my mom concerned and at Christmas she gave me a Fox mini bike that was street legal and had an even bigger engine. I got two moving violations by the same motorcycle cop before I was 15½ then got my learner's permit, making me legal.

Rick and Chocolate

My friend Rick Perez hated this story because it was true. At the time I transferred to Joaquin Miller Junior High, I was 4' 11" and one of the smallest kids in the school. From eighth grade through the ninth I grew 9 inches to my towering height of 5' 8". I did not know any of the kids, as they had all gone to Hollywood Park School with all of their friends. In the cafeteria, I noticed the cool table of guys and went to sit at their table in an empty seat. But I was informed by Rick that I could not sit there, as it was saved for someone else. So, I sat at another table. In talking with my dad about the situation, Dad said again, "You wouldn't worry so much if you knew how little they thought about you." They are not thinking about you other than maybe the laugh they may have gotten out of it. If you want to sit at that table, then introduce yourself and make them friends if that's what you want."

The next day I got to the cafeteria early and sat down at their table. Rick and his friends showed up and told me I could not sit there. I said, "Hi, my name is Tom Cook and I certainly can sit here and if you do not want to sit with me, you can sit at any other table you choose." Begrudgingly, they sat at the table. About three quarters through lunch, Rick went and bought a chocolate milkshake and snuck up on me from behind and poured it over my head. I calmly wiped the ice cream from my head and, borrowing napkins from other guys at the table, wiped my face, neck, and clothes, then I turned to Rick and said, "Did that make you feel better?" He felt a fool in front of his buddies.

The long and short of it is that I made him a lifelong friend, from 8th grade until his death by cancer at 60. In high school, I loved going to Rick's and having his mom's homemade Mexican food with homemade tortillas. I had to be careful not to leave the dinner table because Rick's bother Ramon would spice up my food with hot sauce too hot for me to eat as a joke. After the laugh they had, he would give my hot-spiced plate to his dad.

QUIP: RIGHT FROM WRONG, PART 3: MITIGATING THE RISK

The "You-know-right-from-wrong" quip continued, and when I was 14-15, he changed it a bit by saying, "Now, I know you know right from wrong and I have explained the risk area and explained the consequences, and I know that you will get into the risk area. If you decide to take the risk, then mitigate it or don't do it. Then if you really have questions about what you're going to do, ask yourself this, 'Would I do this if Dad was standing here?'"

Probably not.

As dad would say, "If you are going to take the risk, mitigate it or don't do it." right from wrong part 3, I took it to heart as it made since, not to get caught and I did my best not to get caught even though I was in the risk area

My brother used to pay me to help prepare for and clean up after his parties. We all make mistakes, but when we made a mistake, he got caught. I learned what not to do. You don't put the old glasses in front. You put them in the back where they belong. You don't turn the glasses upside down if they're stored right side up. You put things back where they belong because moms know where everything in the house is and you do not want to leave tracks.

Once we put the old glasses in front, and my brother got caught because some were turned upside down. Years later, when I had a party, I didn't touch the glasses. I got paper cups and threw them away in a neighbor's trash. My brother would sneak booze from their bottles and would add water and get caught. Learning from that, I would wait for them to have a big party and the next morning I would empty the bottles leaving just a little bit because they would not remember from the night before and I never got caught. "Mitigate the risk."

There was a time when I took my Mom's Cadillac out when my parents were gone. I think I was 14. While I was pulling into the driveway to put the car in the garage, my brother stood and watched me and said there was a good chance Mom checked the mileage. So, I jacked up the Cadillac, stuck it in reverse, and took it back to the right mileage.

In my junior year of high school, I took my California license saying I was born in 1948 and scratched off half the 8, making it look like a three, thus making me 21 at 16. I then went to Harrah's Casino and applied for and received my Harrah's courtesy card so I could gamble.

This worked well until Jack Giere and I went to Straw Hat Pizza the night before our high school graduation and ordered a pizza and a pitcher of beer and the service guy who had checked our ID called the cops on us. We were arrested, booked, and jailed, then allowed our one phone call. It was about 3:00 am. I called my mom. She said, "Where are you?

"I am in jail."

"Good. You can stay there." and click went the phone.

"Mom, Mom??"

She showed up the next morning with an attorney. It cost me $110 for that pitcher of beer and $100 for the attorney, which mom made me pay for. But we got out in time to make it to our graduation.

My high school never had my parents' signatures; it was only mine. I signed everything. Every note that my mom ever gave me, I rewrote in my own hand. So, all the handwriting they ever had was mine. If I wanted to cut school, I just wrote my own excuse. Until one day, two weeks before graduating, they called and I got caught even though I had it set up. I did not abuse it and only cut school a couple of times during high school.

During and after high school was the hippy 60s with long hair. Most of our friends had long hippy hair but Chris and I had short all-American frat boy hair cuts. Like Dad said, "Don't be classed as a hippy." "Why look the part?" especially if you were holding. I ate the roaches to eliminate any tracks.

Always trying to mitigate the risks.

Getting Set for Life: Approval, Recognition, and Encouragement

At 14, I was working for Dad's construction company in the cabinet shop and mowing lawns at the model homes. There was a drafting person working on plans at the model home and it intrigued me. With my first paycheck, I bought a drafting board, T square, & triangles and tried drawing plans. I received recognition from Dad because he could not draw a straight line. I started taking drafting classes and then in college thought I wanted to be an architect, but then realized I was not top of the class material.

Because I had been in construction from 12 years old, I went into the construction business and we paid talented architects to do the plans we wanted to build. Because of recognition and exposure to construction and real estate, I was fortunate as a young man to have an idea that I would be in construction and real estate as my career. But it was Dad's recognition and encouragement of my interest in drafting and drawing that lead me to pursue the education that ended up being a very big asset to me, that knowledge combined with construction. I gained the experience over the years.

Christian Brothers School

After Joaquin Miller 8th grade, I changed to Christian Brothers located in the original school at 21st and Broadway, which was later condemned, so I only went for one year then on to C. K. McClatchy. But what a year with the brothers. Things were really different then. My home room was 222 with Brother Justin and he was great. We had a great time, but boy did you toe the line and you learned quickly how things work.

Just as an example, one day, I was studying history in Brother Owen's English class. He snuck up, grabbed the book and threw it across the classroom to the corner and two points into the trash can. I popped off and said "Those books cost money and I am going to tell the principle." "You're damned right you're going to tell the principle." He grabbed me by the lapel of my coat, jerked me up and out of the seat, pushed me down the row and towards the door and while doing so, he clipped my shoe off as he shoved me out the door leaving me standing in the hallway.

While I am standing there, the Brother teaching across the hall with his door open said to the class "Excuse me, gentlemen." He walked out of his class across the hall, pointed his finger at me and said, "Don't ever let me catch you out in the hall without both shoes on." He turned and went back to his class.

Twenty minutes later, the bell rang ending English class. I retrieved my books, headed down the stairs to Mr. Gracitas's history class, and walked in. I was pissed off and slammed my books down on the desk top as I slouched into my seat. Then I heard in a loud voice, "Get up, you clown." "Cook, I am talking to you. Get up and come in here as a gentleman." So, I picked up my books and went out of the classroom then re-entered. He was standing in front of my row. When I went to pass, he knocked the books out of my hands and said, "You didn't say, 'excuse me.' Try again." I tried again and when I said, "Excuse me" to pass, he said "Go around." Brother Owen met me after the class and said, "Don't do history in my English class." "OK," I said.

At Christian Brothers, if you got into a fight, they would take the two that were fighting to the gym and put gloves on them to fight if they still wanted to with nobody around. I had Brother Justin for homeroom and religion. In the first week, he wanted us to prove to him that there was a God! The class tried and tried. He said you guys sound like a bunch of parrots reciting you catechism—start thinking.

We spent the whole week with little progress, then he laid out 10 explanations. I don't remember them but hung on to two of them. The first one was there had to be a first mover (GOD) and the last one was "you need to have faith."

QUIP: RIGHT FROM WRONG, PART 4: I CAN'T BE WITH YOU

The "You-know-right-from-wrong" quip was backed up in Dad's sermons, but the most important part of the quip is "I CAN'T BE WITH YOU." Because he wasn't. His sermons made it clear that I was on your my own; I had been given all the freedom with very few boundaries. He made it clear that I was responsible for my choices, behavior, and actions because he can't be with me. You are responsible for making your own life. "Take care of yourself and you will take care of everyone around you." I had plenty of unsupervised freedom with no boundaries and could go anywhere and do just about anything I wanted to do. And although I pulled some shenanigans and risky business, I could have gotten much further into major trouble. I didn't because his words and teachings created this invisible wall at the edge of the cliff of disaster. I was always pushing the limits, but only so far.

QUIP: WHAT IF AND THEN WHAT?

This one ties into mitigating the risk. It was just another tool to make you think and plan and maybe not do something because the answer is not worth the risk. It not only applied to pushing the limits as a kid, but it was also about planning steps to succeeding on a project or a goal and helped crystalize my thinking and planning by asking the question, "what if, "and "then what?" Major life decisions and paths can be clearer by asking yourself **what if** and **then what.**

Cadillac Rabbit Chasing

My mom had a new 1963 turquoise Fleetwood Cadillac: d. It had the big fins on the back fenders of the car. My friends and I went rabbit chasing in that car in an area of Sacramento known as the pocket area, which at that time was farms and agriculture but now is known as Greenhaven. We used to drive out there, drink beer, take our bows, and go rabbit hunting; we'd sit on the front of the car and go looking for rabbits in the headlights.

So, we got a little drunk one night. We started chasing them in my mom's Cadillac in this flat field, and we were going when all of a sudden, there was this Boom! We hit a mound of dirt. We were kind of airborne for a moment. After stopping the car, we discovered it was one of those irrigation ditches that divide the fields and we ended up in another field. The only one way to get out of that field was to go back the way you came, back over the ditch. So I went back over the ditch, washed the car, and took it home.

Three days later, she took it in for service because the oil light came on. When she picked it up, the service man said to my mom, "What did you run over?" She said, "What do you mean?" He said, "Your oil pan has this big dent in it and there was a little hole causing the oil leak. So, what did you hit?" She said she didn't hit anything. When she got home, she told me about it. I said, "Well, I may have accidently hit one of those curbs in the parking lot. I'm sorry."

LAND LEASE

When I was 17, the family had a piece of property on the corner of Franklin Blvd. and Florin Road, right next to Cal Worthington Chevrolet. But when I was a kid, I used to ride my bike out to the property and play out there. The front half, from Franklin Blvd. back, was leased to the Japanese farmers. Behind that was a large barn and a small fenced-in construction yard. The barn had been used for the cabinet shop when they built the Bowling Green subdivision. The little construction yard was where they parked the trucks.

From time to time, I would ride my bike out there to play, then when I could drive, we started buying jalopies and taking them out to the barn where we were playing demolition derby, crashing through stacked log rounds and racing around the back acreage.

We had an English Ford that had no engine or anything. It was just four wheels and a shell; we had a drive shaft as our roll bar. We would push this car with another jalopy, trying to make a 90-degree turn in the mud. We wore football helmets for safety. We were out there doing this one time, and two gentlemen came up. They wanted to lease the little construction yard to wreck cars. I said, "Well, that is fine. I will lease the construction yard to you." I leased it to them for $125 a month. Well, in 1965, that was equivalent to rent on a very nice four-bedroom, two-bath home in a good area.

Fast forward a year and a half later. I came through the side kitchen door and my mom said, "You better go see your dad." Into the living room I went. My dad was sitting in his big, green, leather chair. He said, "I understand that you leased the Bowling Green land, is that correct?"

I said, "Aw, yes."

And he said, "Well, what did you lease?"

I said, "The little construction yard."

He said, "What kind of rent are you getting?"

I said, "$125 a month."

"A month?" he asked.

"Yes, per month," I replied.

"How long you been doing that?"

I lied and said, "A little over a year."

He said, "That's fine. I want the money."

"Dad. I don't have the money."

He said, "Well, what gives you the right to lease land that's not yours?"

I said, "It's ours."

He says, "But it's not yours."

"But it's still ours!!"

"No, it is not," he said in a raised voice.

I said, "The land is not ours?"

He said, "No. The land is not ours nor is it mine."

I said, "If you don't own the land, who owns the land?"

He said, "It's your Uncle George's."

My Uncle George hadn't been out to the property for some time, but when he went out there, he found those guys wrecking cars on his land. "Uh, what are you doing on my property wrecking cars?" he asked.

They said, "We have a lease."

"You have a lease? May I see the lease?"

The guys gave my Uncle George the lease. Of course, he turned it over to my dad, so my dad read me the riot act and sent me to my room. My mom was coming out of the kitchen and we passed each other. I hadn't gotten down the bedroom hall far enough to where I was out of earshot when I heard my mom say, "Well Bill, how did that go?" My dad said, "Isn't that the greatest thing you have ever heard of? The kid's 17 and leasing land and look at this document. He has every provision covered."

Many years later, I was having lunch with my Uncle George and I said, "You never said anything to me about me leasing your land out at Bowling Green. He looked up at me and said, "I have 12 children and I just don't get excited. Plus, I knew your dad would take care of it."

My Uncle George, you talk about class, he was the best of the bunch, lived to be 92, was married 72 years to my Aunt Jane, had 12 children and accepted and treated me as one of their own. A true example of character. Then years later, my brother and I bought this property from Uncle George and built a R&D development known as 7000 Franklin Blvd.

Quip: Be Good

Mom was the one who always talked about my guardian angel and listening to the voice in my right ear. I didn't always listen because I was going to do what I wanted to do despite what the voice might be saying or warning. In high school, when I left for a date or other activity, Mom would say, "Be good and if you can't be good, be careful. If you can't be careful, you better stay home."

Cook-King Casinos

When we were juniors in high school, my friend Chris King and I were heading to his bedroom, which was directly behind the garage, when I noticed a folded up, green felt blanket. In the corner of the fold, I saw a big 6 and a big 8 printed on the green felt. I knew exactly what it was because my dad was a big craps player and at Christmas time, my family played craps after dinner. When we were tall enough to see over the table and had money, we could play. So, we played craps from the time we were old enough to see above the table.

I said, "Chris, Is that a craps cloth?" He said it was his grandfather's cloth from Harrah's Club. I unfolded the cloth out there in the garage and it was a regulation-sized craps tablecloth with the Harrah's club logo in the middle. I said, "Wow. Let's build a table."

Eddie Meda, who lived next door to Chris, was good at woodworking and had the tools and skills, so we had him help us build a regulation-sized craps table. We used waffle-patterned carpet padding as the padded side wall railing. We had chip rails on the top rail and a casino chip station. After completing it, we put it down in Chris's basement. One night, we were having a small party and I said, "Hey, Chris, let's open up the table."

So, we opened the table with just our friends there at the party, and we made $35.

I said, "Well, that is pretty good. Let's have a little bit bigger party."

So, we had a little bit bigger party and we made $75. But the basement wasn't big enough to handle anymore people. I told Chris, "Why don't we kick this up a couple notches and move the operation over to my parents' garage."

My parents were always over in Hawaii on business. We had a very large two-car garage with a storage room that we used as our back bar storage room and a laundry room next to it that we used as a cashier's station. My mom was storing Helen Giere's carpet from down the street, which we rolled halfway across the floor of the garage and then hung it in front of the doors so no sound would get out. We had a shuttle bus from the Raley's parking lot. It cost $5 to get into the bus, and we gave people $5 worth of coded chips. That way, there was no noise, no cars, and no party evidence, thereby mitigating the risk. We didn't want to get caught running an illegal gambling casino. In the casino, we added two blackjack tables, a roulette table, the regulation-sized craps table, and a bar.

To keep anyone from counterfeiting our plain plastic chips from night to night, every time we opened, we coded the chips with different colors. So, if the previous time $1 chip was yellow, for the next time, we'd put a penny on it and spray it orange. Then, we had an orange chip with a yellow dot. They couldn't be counterfeited. The final night's chips are in the possession of Bobby Houston whose parents bought the Parkridge house from us when my mom sold it. The chips were still hanging in the garage when the house changed possession and he still has them today.

We were always trying to figure out how to get booze, but we were only 16 and 17. We tried the taxicab when Dad was in the shower. That never worked. We had some people who would buy it, but it was such a hassle at Red Fox Liquors on Martin Luther King Blvd. to try and get someone to buy us booze. But one day, I was walking down the hallway when I heard my dad on the phone in his den, saying, "Willie, this is Bill Cook. I'd like a fifth of Jack Daniels, a fifth of vodka and some mix. . Deliver it to the outside refrigerator and stick it on my bill. Thanks, Willie." Click went the receiver and Bingo went off in my head. Three days later, I called the Hollywood Bottle Shop and I said, "Willie, this is Bill Cook. I want two cases of Olympia beer and a couple six packs of coke and a six-pack of

7-Up. Deliver it to the outside refrigerator and stick it on my bill. Thanks, Willie." Click. Three hours later, vroom, there it is in our outside fridge. So, a couple of days later, I went down to the Hollywood Bottle Shop and I said my dad sent me in to pay part of his bill. Then I paid my bill. Willie didn't care; he couldn't get caught because it was for Bill Cook.

So, we moved the casino to my parents' garage. Over the next couple years, we opened five maybe six times there. We averaged $1,200 to $1,500 a night, net. We decided again that we were going to kick it up a couple notches. Chris went down to the Jointed Cue, at 24th and FruitRidge, and invited Robby Nakamura and our Asian friends to the casino.

That evening, as we were in the process of getting ready for this bigger event, unloading $1,200 worth of liquor, beer kegs, ice, and mix out of the Hollywood Bottle Shop's delivery van, up drove the Yellow Cab with my parents in it. I handed off the case of liquor to one of the other guys and went back and said, "Hi, Mom. Hi, Dad. Let me help you with the luggage." I grabbed a couple of bags, and as we were walking towards the side gate that led to the breezeway, I said, "Mom, we're going to have a little party."

She said, "Well, yeah, I can kind of see that." I said, "Don't worry about anything. We're going to have it in the garage." She said, "Oh, that's nice. Well, I want to see the garage." Then she made that right-hand turn through the storage room and ended up going through the door into the garage. Next to her was her large chest freezer, but on top of that freezer was the stair step of all the bottles and glasses. She ended up standing behind the bar, overlooking this casino with two blackjack tables, a craps table, a roulette wheel and a bar. My mom didn't normally swear, but she said, "Oh, shit. You can't gamble!" I said, "Mom, don't worry about a thing. It's all chips."

Unbeknownst to me, the cops had come to the door that night because someone had called due to all the cars parked for the party, but my parents took care of it. We had neglected to have the guys from the Jointed Cue use the shuttle bus, which gave the party away and broke my rule of mitigating the risk.

At another point, at about 2:00 am, the five guys playing blackjack wanted us to take the limits off the table. When we agreed, they all slapped down $100 each. Chris looked at the $500 dollars on the table knowing that our bank was $1,500 plus chips sold in the bus or at the cashier. So, Chris said we could not open the limits to that much money, but we agreed to do so for three hands. Our gambling friend Larry Smith dealt for us that night. When the first hand was dealt, Larry was showing a 2 and all five players were standing pat.

Dealer pulled out a buried king then drew a 9 for 21 and the casino took everyone's money. Chris took a small sigh of relief. Then Larry dealt the second hand and again they all bet $100; this time, the dealer showed a 3. They all stood pat. Chris took a big breath and gave me the look, then the dealer drew to 20, pushed with two players and took $300 from the other three. The third hand was dealt and once again, they all bet $100 dollars and stood pat. Dealer drew to a 19, paid one winner, pushed with one and beat 3 for another $300. I don't know if it was just luck or if Larry was somehow pulling the right cards from the deck; he was a pro card player.

Long and short of it is that my mom stayed up with us until 8:30 the next morning when we shut it down. My dad lost $470 in IOUs on the craps table before I cut him off and sent him to bed. The next night I went in, I sat down on the edge of the sofa nearest his chair, pulled out all the signed IOUs, laid them on the coffee table in front of him and looking right at him, I said, "Dad, you owe me $470." He sat back in his chair and after a moment, he said, "I think we will just consider that rent on the garage." I said, "Dad, I knew that was coming." That night was our best night; we made $3,800 net. To put this into perspective, in 1968, you could buy a new Corvette out the door and still have money left over. Big night!

In today's world, that would be a $50,000 night in high school.

The 100-Horse Merc

We were 18 or 19 years old at this point, and I had moved out of the house into my first apartment. Chris was a good championship water skier. He wanted to buy a ski boat. We could afford the boat, but we couldn't afford the motor. So, we spotted this 100-horse Mercury on a boat down at the Sacramento River marina. I think it was Millers Landing. We had been kind of fantasizing about getting inner tubes, tying them to the engine, and dropping the thing into the river, thinking we could then float it down the river. Had we tried this, it would have gone straight to the bottom.

At Easter, we went out and got drunk and then decided, not even considering the risks, with a pair of pliers and a pair of vice grips, we were going to get that motor. A little after 2:00 am, we went to a cove down from the marina. Now, remember it was Easter, still a little cold. We took off our clothes, swam up to the marina, and grabbed the boat. We brought it back down to the cove, then we started to disconnect the cables to get the motor off the boat. Well, a 100-horse Merc weighs, I think, about 980 pounds. We hadn't really taken this into consideration.

We got the screws and cable disconnected and we got the bolts that held the motor to the back of the boat undone. We were trying to lift it three inches to get it clear of the back rail of the boat. Well, lifting 980 pounds was not that easy, but we did manage to get it up high enough to clear the mount.

As soon as it got up high enough, it fell straight at me and took me to the bottom of the river, landing on my arm and pinning me to the bottom. It was about 3:00 in the morning and pitch black. We did not have a flashlight and I was pinned by this 900-pound engine at the bottom of the river, and I couldn't get out. But when I reached my left hand up, my fingertips were just barely breaking the surface of the water. So, I start splashing at the water, Chris, Chris. I was splashing around, splashing around. Chris, Chris, Chris. I am right here! He jumped out of the boat, grabbed my arm and started pulling on it. The mud was just soft enough to where I slipped out from underneath the 900 lb. behemoth.

We spent the next three hours trying to get that engine up that levee one inch at a time, then rolled it down the backside just as the sun was coming up on Riverside Boulevard. We lugged the huge, 100-horse Merc into my MGB. Then we scooted off to my apartment and put it into the apartment closet.

Directly after the heist, we discovered that we could not buy new controls, which we left in the boat, because we had to give them the serial number on the engine to purchase new controls. We couldn't do that. So, the thing sat around for a couple of years. Chris finally sold it and, because it had been in the water and never run and everything, it was no good. And then we found out that the boat owner was happy as a lark because the engine had some real damage to it before we stole it.

Box of Dirt

When I was 19 almost 20 years old, my parents were in Hawaii on business with the Savings and Loan. It was Christmas, and I was over at my brother's house where I received a present from my parents. When I opened it, it was a shoebox, and it was full of dirt. My dad was famous for giving presents that had symbolism to them. And because it was a box of dirt, I knew exactly what it was. It meant land! I immediately started digging into the dirt, and I pulled out the plat map for the Parkway Greens subdivision. At the top of the plat map it said, "Merry Christmas. You are entitled to one lot of your choice."

After a couple of days had gone by, my brother Bill said, "What lot do you want?"

"Well, I want that one, on the corner."

"Yeah? What are you going to do with it?"

"I am going to build a duplex on it."

"What are you going to do? Wait for Dad to get home?"

"Well, I was thinking about it."

"Well, if you do, what do you think he is going to say?"

I said, "Well, he's going to ask me what lot do I want and what am I going to do with it. And then he'll say, 'Don't talk about it. Do it.'"

My brother suggested I get a head start on it.

Good idea.

I took engineering drafting in high school and was an architectural major at city college. I went home, set up my drafting board, got out my T-square and triangles and spent the next two weeks or so drawing a full set of plans for a 3,600 square foot, hipped-roof duplex. Three bedrooms, two baths on each side. After I completed the plans, I took them to Brownie's Blueprint and had them printed up. Then, with Mark Ures's help I delivered the plans to the various subcontractors for pricing, and I completed my lumber and materials list. Then I went to the Bank of America for the loan and cost breakdown forms, collected my subcontractor bids, filled out all the forms, put it in a file, and stuck it on my desk, waiting for my parents to come home.

A few days after my parents had arrived home, I walked into the living room where Dad was sitting in his green, leather chair. I remember I had a charcoal-colored corduroy coat on. I went in and I said, "Dad, I really want to thank you for the lot."

He said, "Oh, you're welcome. Which one do you want?"

Without hesitating, I reached inside the lapel of my coat, and I pulled out the plat map of the subdivision. I laid it on the coffee table and pointed to the one I chose.

He said, "Ah, that's good. That's a nice lot. What do you want to put on it?"

I said, "I am going to build a duplex on it so I can have rental income to help pay the majority of the loan payments." We had a discussion about loans, interest rates and ability to make the payments, and the numbers worked.

He said, "That's not a bad idea; in concept it seems to work but the costs need to be verified. So, if you want to do this, don't talk about it. Do it."

I said, "I understand but excuse me for a second." I went back to my room, got my full set of plans and file, brought it into the living room, and dropped it on the coffee table. I said, "Take it to the bank tomorrow."

His mouth dropped open as if he had seen a ghost. He opened up the full set of plans and looked through it carefully. Then he opened up the file, and it was all filled out. The cost breakdown was done, all the forms were ready to take to the bank. He then looked up at me and said, "Don't you think this is a little bit big?"

I leaned forward and looked right at him and I said, "Dad, if you can build a small one, you can build a big one there is just more of it." Shortly after that, I had my loan and started building the duplex.

It took almost seven months to complete, but I built it by myself with help from time to time. What an education I received by building this duplex. Although I had worked in construction since I was 12, I had never constructed a whole house. By this time, I had been around construction for several years doing labor work on every area of the construction, along with some framing and carpentry. A year or so prior to this, I had the opportunity to meet and work for my mentor, Mark L. Ures. What a great man. I received a real education in construction and life from him.

My dad knew I had not built anything myself but still allowed me to proceed. He did not want to show his concerns, so he had one of his partners and friend Billy Walker build a house two lots down the street. That way Billy could watch me and report back to my dad how I was progressing. I had a lot of input and help from Mark Ures, especially with the hip roof. I could not have done it without his help.

It came out really nice. Although I had originally planned on moving into one side of the duplex, the Army got in the way. I rented both sides for a number of years, then sold it.

ONE OF MY OWN QUIPS: TOMORROW WILL BE A BETTER DAY

This one originated as a self-survival tool to get me through the turmoil that occurred in the house due to Dad's drinking. It was my tool to keep a positive attitude and get through the night, that **"Tomorrow will be a better day."** In most cases it was, until the next episode. I have used this self-produced quip and wisdom so many times during my life to help me get past many bad days.

Making Sense: The Rest of

the

Story

When I tell three, maybe four, of my stories around a campfire, they're pretty cool stories, but when you put them all down in black and white on a page in sequential order, the picture that emerges from between the lines of the stories is not pretty. Who was this entrepreneurial, out-of-control, traveling-at-the-speed-of-sound, pushing-the-limits-while-trying-to-fly-level kid and what made him that way? And how did he survive? Well, if I knew the answer to that, I would be a billionaire.

I assume it comes from a combination of many factors, but I think environmental mentors and teachers are big shapers. Everyone experiences life's hardships and dysfunctions, some more than others. Although we lived in a very nice house, the home was dysfunctional in that we didn't operate as a family. Mom always fed us first because dad always worked late. We had dinner as a family twice a year: Christmas and Thanksgiving. Looking back, as a young kid, I solved that by adopting other families; I was always at one of my friend's houses: The Gieres, the Reids, the Meretts and many others. My friend Robert Dewant and his family did many neat things, and I joined them when I was around 10: Yosemite, Lake Tahoe, and camping. Robert's dad Randy always made wheat germ waffles on Sunday mornings. They operated as a family and I liked that.

Then came high school when we were busy with our own lives, friends, school, and fraternity functions. I had a great time in high school. In Sacramento, we had high school fraternities and sororities and after 50 years, we still get together at Jack Giere's Christmas party. After high school, I met Mark L. Ures through his daughter Dana whom I was dating and later engaged. I spent almost two and a half years with Dana and her great family. During that time, I fell in love with her father Mark as a teacher and a mentor. What a great man, and I appreciate the opportunity I had to know him. I vitally needed his examples, his wisdom, his work ethic and family life style because I was lost. Some of his quips, which I use all the time, were "Let me show you a trick I learned in the old country," "don't sweat the small shit," and "I have no problem with your work as long as it is perfect!" just to name a few.

As a child, I was not aware of my dad's alcohol problem until I was about 11. My brother and I were well aware of the drinking prior to this, but it wasn't evident to me as to the actual degree of the disease. Mom did her best to control the situation, but she was also a good co-alcoholic. From 11 years old on, things progressed and deteriorated quickly. I will not go into all the awful details or events that occurred during the subsequent 12 years and the disruption and drama that occurred. This is where I used my personal survival technique and an optimistic view that **"tomorrow will be a better day."** In most cases, that was true. But having an alcoholic in the house is like an elephant showing up every so often causing turmoil.

My brother was soon off to college, leaving just my mom and me. As the years went on and things got worse, I became Dad's watcher. I was the one who tracked him down, pulled him from the bars, and broke up the fights. I came home one evening, and Mom and Dad were sitting in the living room with their pitcher of martinis on the side table next to Dad's chair when Mom said, "Chris is waiting for you in your bedroom." I went to get him but he wasn't there. I said to myself out loud, "Hum, I wonder where he is." Then I heard him say, "I am right here." I forget if he was under the bed or hiding in the closet but I said, "What are you doing?" He said, "Your parents were having a huge fight and it scared me." I said it was no big deal, as it happened all the time. Let's go to the party. This is called shell shock where you get accustomed to the outrages. Tomorrow will be a better day.

One time, while at the cabin with my mom, my dad agreed to go to an alcoholic rehab in Redwood City. I drove from Sacramento to the cabin near Tahoe then drove to the Bay Area where dad talked me into stopping for dinner at Vanessa's on Broadway in San Francisco on the way; he knew I couldn't pass that up, as it was one of my favorite San Francisco restaurants. Then he went to the bathroom and ditched me. It took me two hours to find him and get him back into the car to take him to the rehab facility in Redwood City. I checked him into the rehab and took his wallet, cash, and clothes. I drove home stopping at my girlfriend's house for a few minutes. I walked through the living room and dining room door, and there he was, sitting in his green leather chair still in his hospital gown with drink to his side, flipping me the bird.

Quip: Take care of yourself and you will take care of everyone around you.

This was another quip that was repeated periodically and it came up again when I was building the duplex. The translation ties back into almost all the quips and that is, you are responsible for you and if you take care of you, then you will take care of the people around you. I think he did this because he was leaving the house and my mom, and he knew he would not be around for me: you are on your own. I was 20 at the time and he didn't return except for a few times until I was 30.

This was the point when everyone gave up on Dad. Some years later after my parents' divorce, he remarried, but he was still drinking. His new wife could not keep up with the drinking, so she decided to quit and got sober herself. She then helped Dad get sober shortly thereafter. He remained sober for the next 25+ years until his death from cancer. By the time he had gotten sober, we had completed the first office project and moved from Dad's old office downtown to our new office building and changed the name of the company to "The Cook Company," leaving Dad behind.

After getting sober, he wanted to come work in the office, but my brother would have no part of it and said NO. Thereafter, he sold his Sutter Creek Ranch and moved to Hawaii for about two and half years, when he returned to Sacramento. My brother would have nothing to do with him, so I provided him with an office and secretarial support for his real estate dealings in my office for the next 25 years. Because of the dismantling of my grandfather's company upon his death and the 15-20 plus years he lost in the business world, he could never recapture his hey days.

Shortly after my mom's divorce, we sold the Parkridge house and moved Mom to the Mark III apartments that I had helped build when working for my mentor Mark Ures. The next number of years was not the happiest time. She was out of the Parkridge house in a small apartment, and her boys were now busy with work and their families. Several years later, she married Jack Skinner, vice president of Bank of America, and life became happier and normal, which was much better.

Becoming an Adult

Prior to my graduating in 1966, the Vietnam War was starting to heat up as we became sophomores. All of us kids were very patriotic, proud Americans. We were gung ho kids, especially the kids in classes ahead of us. I called them The 4th of July Boys because they went to war willingly, without really knowing what was up. My classmates and I really didn't know what was happening either. We had the draft and when you were 18, you were drafted into the Army. So as we were coming up through the years, what started to happen in the news and what was really happening in Vietnam started to become clear, verified by the body bags showing up on the tarmac.

At the time, we were looking down the barrel of Vietnam. When you graduated you are going to 'Nam. The resistance to the war was starting to develop. By the time we were seniors, people were thinking, what are we going to do? Go to Canada? Get married? Go to college? How are we going to avoid the draft and the war was really the key question. It was the fuel that powered all of the demonstrations and history against the war. The classes of '65 and '66 were the leading edge of the revolt and demonstrations and everything that took place in the mid to late 1960s.

The country was in turmoil; just prior to the war, we had the civil rights issue and protests. When news of the discrimination in the south of black people hit home, I was blindsided and outraged. What do you mean they have separate bathrooms, drinking fountains and have to ride in the back of the bus? You have got to be kidding me. We don't treat people that way here in the United States. Do we? How can that be? But it was true! We had Black people who were friends like family.

I loved Martin Luther King, Jr. and all that he accomplished for the good of the people and country. Within his "I have a dream speech," he made a statement "I look to a day when people will not be judged by the color of their skin, but by the content of their character." Content of character is an important quality of all people. If you have content of character, there is no judgment on color.

The Army Story

After graduation, to avoid the draft, I went to Sacramento City College and was carrying the 14.5 units required to keep me from being drafted. After the first year, I transferred to Lane Community College because I was trying to get into the University of Oregon for an architectural program. When I flunked my Psych 1 class, it dropped me below the required units. After some time, Uncle Sam sent a notification to report to the Oakland induction center.

About 9 months prior to receiving my induction notice, I was leaving to go home from the Laguna Sea races at Fort Ord with my girlfriend Dana. There was a straightaway with a large Army truck in front of me going about 15 mph. It was clear and I went to pass, when all of a sudden, he turned left into a field in front of me. I went right underneath his gas tank and into a front wheel, just mangling that MGB.

It was a good thing we had our seat belts on or we would have been dead. Even with the lap belt, I still crushed the steering wheel, cracked the windshield with my head and hurt my back slightly. So, I started using my back as my basis for seeing orthopedic specialists and to educate myself about having a bad back in hopes of using it to get a 4-F rating before I was called up by Uncle Sam to report to the Oakland induction center. Because it was the Army's fault for the accident, two service men came to the house to meet with my mom and dad to take care of the damage and confirm that we were not suing. I told Dad it was a great time to negotiate a 4-F rating to keep me from going to 'Nam. He tried, but it was out of their control.

I reported to the Oakland induction center and, like every other good American kid, I arrived in the absolute worst condition I could be in, right? People were doing every conceivable thing to get out of being drafted. There were guys wearing pink lace panties and swallowing tin foil to make it look like ulcers, contaminating their urine samples and I mean, everything you can imagine doing, they were doing it. I tried flunking the hearing test, and it didn't work. I am as blind as a bat and that didn't make any difference.

They gave me a classification of 2-B. I was looking on the back of my draft card as I was coming down the stairs. I said, what the hell is a 2-B? I asked the guy at the last station, "What is a classification of 2-B?"

He said, "To be drafted. Have you been arrested?"

I said, "Yes."

He said, "Go over to the Group W bench."

What a day, and the thoughts were "Wow, I am going to be drafted. I am going to 'Nam. If I go to 'Nam, I am not coming home. This is not a good thing. What am I going to do now?" Ever since the car accident in Fort Ord, my goal was to use it to get out of the Army. I went to a civilian doctor for my bad back from the accident to start building a medical file to obtain a 4-F draft rating. That didn't work.

So much for the 4-F classification. After receiving a 2-B draft classification, my brother was working on getting me into the Army Reserves. He had some friends and pulled strings and he got me into the 91st Division Army Bagpipe Band. I wore a kilt. That was fine with me. I learned how to play tenor drum really quickly. The band part of it was really fun. We didn't get paid for it, and we still had to do the Reserve meetings.

Within the first six months, they wanted to send me off to basic training. I said they couldn't send me because I was building the duplex on the land my dad had given me. I had it in the frame stage and I could not leave the project at that stage. They didn't send me to basic training for a year and a half. I used this time and two summer camps at Fort Ord to educate myself on the workings of the Army and the dispensary and to paper my medical file in preparation for basic, then they sent me to Fort Lewis, Washington for my basic training.

I had told all my friends when I left that I would be home early.

They had looked at me and said, "Yeah. Um-hmm."

"No, trust me. I'll be home early."

"Yeah, sure you will."

Before I get into the basic training part of the story, I need to apologize for my planned behavior. It was not to offend the military or its personnel; it was part of my plan and strategy for getting out of the Army, as I was not an Army kind of guy. Remember, at the time, the whole country was against the war and it was not a volunteer army. Also, the timing could not have been better for implementing my plan. For years leading up to this point, there had been all the demonstrations against the war resulting in the shooting at Kent State. the mothers of America were all over the Senate and the House to lighten up on the abuse of the troops and training because too many were dying in the process. The Senate had started coming down hard on the Army to be much less aggressive.

I have much respect for our military and the people who volunteer to serve and protect us, which is the main function of the Government.

When I went to Fort Lewis for basic, I not only had my medical file but also had a full back brace strapped to me like a corset. During the first week when we were getting our shots and I had taken my shirt off revealing the back brace, my drill sergeant came over and asked what the hell that was. I told him I had a bad back and it was my back brace. He just walked away.

I didn't go to basic training in my civilian clothes. I only took my Army uniforms. Everybody else arrived from Timbuktu and wherever in the country in their civvies. I already had my uniform on. In addition to that, I am legally blind without my glasses. I took prescription dark glasses with me. That first night, they woke us up at 4:30 and marched us down to the barbershop and shaved all our hair off. Then we couldn't find our friends from the night before. They tear you down and take everything away, but there is one thing they cannot take away from you; that is your personality. Because I was already Army, they made me platoon guide of the 1st Platoon. In the first week, we, the new trainees, went through what I called Reception Camp, which is where you got your uniform, you got your shots, you learned how to march and peel potatoes and maybe pulled a little KP.

After they got us all situated, we went to the companies and started basic training. I was platoon guide of the 1st Platoon, so I led the entire Alpha Company, 200 guys, up to start basic training at the barracks. Now, the barracks was a three-story building laid out where there was the supply room downstairs in the basement. Ground floor level was permanent party housing, offices, mess hall, and game room. Second floor was 1st and 2nd Platoons. Third floor was 3rd and 4th Platoons with a separating white line across the hall. We did not cross that line if we were in 2 or 3, you know, we just didn't cross it. There were five or six of these buildings that housed companies of trainees in basic training. There were about a thousand young men in training.

Because I was a platoon guide of the first platoon, I was leading the entire Alpha Company up to the entry steps and the Captain was standing on the stoop of the steps; he saw me coming. Finally, he could read my nametag. When I got up to him, he said, "Cook, where are you going?"

"I'm going to basic training, sir."

He shook his head a little bit and said, "Where are you going?"

"I am going to basic training, sir."

He said, "What is all this shit?" referring to my 91st Division Army patch, Private 1st Class stripes, Powder River pins, and nametag. Compared to everybody else, I looked like a permanent party.

I said, "Oh, I am in the Army Reserves."

And he said, "Oh, that's fine. It all comes off."

I said, "No, Sir. I suggest you look it up under section 15-709. 'You earn it. You keep it.'" However, shortly thereafter, they did come off.

This set him back and he got a little flustered. He looked at me and said, "The dark glasses. They got to go."

I said, "No, sir. I am legally blind without my glasses. Until I get Army issue, these are the only ones I have."

He said, "Move on." We proceeded to our assigned barracks. So that night, about 9:00, we went downstairs into the supply room and walked down the ramp of the loading dock to the single-man door. We stood in the door at a relaxed attention called parade rest until we were called to get our bedding. When I got to the door with my dark glasses on, it was 9:00 at night. I could see the supply sergeant in my peripheral view to the right. I heard him say, "Hey, Bee-bop." I knew he was talking to me, but I didn't pay any attention to him. I just kept looking straight ahead. "Hey, Bee-bop. Hey Bee-bop. I am talking to you, Bee-bop." Then I saw him get up from his desk, this guy was probably 6' 3", 270 pounds. He was huge. He came from around his desk and briskly walked up to me. He stuck his Smokey the Bear hat under the brim of my cap and said in this deep low and slow voice, "Heeeey, Bee-bop. I am talking to you."

I said, "Supply Sergeant, I address you as Supply Sergeant, and when you address me as Private Cook, I will answer you because my name is not Bee-bop."

He took me over to his desk and asked, "What did you do in civilian life?"

"I'm a builder."

"Well, how many people do you have working for you?"

"Oh, I don't know, one or two from time to time."

"Oh, not a very big company, is it?"

I said, "No, it's not. But I guarantee you one thing. I made a lot more money than being in the Army." With that, I got dismissed.

We got back up to the barracks, made our beds, organized our foot lockers, and went off to sleep. The next morning, I got up late because I tried to squeeze that last five minutes of sleep. I was kind of rushing. I ran into the shower quickly. When I got back to my bunk, my bed was made. I said, "All right. Who made my bed?"

The guy in the bunk above me said, "I made it."

"Well, why in the hell did you make my bed?"

"Because last night you stuck up for me, and nobody has stuck up for me in my life. And that is why I made your bed."

"Cool. Thanks."

I don't remember what I did to earn that; I guess somebody was in his face. I just stepped up in their face and told them, "Knock it off."

Next morning, I got out of the shower, went back to my bunk, and my bed was made. I said, "Hey, pal. You don't need to make my bed, you know. I mean, I understand the first time, but you don't need to do that."

He said, "You know what? It's not a problem for me."

"Hey, pal, you want to make my bed? Make my bed."

I didn't make my bed in the Army until I was transferred to the holdover barrack.

We completed the first week of training and on Sunday, 1st Brigadier General's inspection happened. I was platoon guide of the 1st Platoon; 1st Platoon ate last in the first week, and Platoon Leader ate last of his platoon, so I was the last guy to eat. It wasn't enough time to get my food, eat and be back in formation. The General worked his way down the line of troops standing at attention asking each, "How's the food?"

"Fine, sir."

"Get enough to eat?"

"Yes, sir."

"How's the food?"

"Fine, sir."

"Get enough to eat?"

"Yes, sir."

He got to me. "How's the food?"

"Fine, sir."

"Get enough to eat?"

"No, sir."

And when I said, "No sir," you could see the troops up and down the barracks just thinking, oh, no, what is he doing now? There was a wave that went through the troops standing at attention.

He was almost two guys down from me before he realized that I had said no. And he came back and said, "No, sir?"

And I said, "No, sir."

"Why not?"

I said, "Well, I am platoon guide of the 1st Platoon. We eat last. I eat last in my platoon. I have five minutes from the time I pick up my tray to eat. It's not enough time."

He said, "Who is your Drill Sergeant?"

"Drill Sergeant Sloan."

He whipped around in his military fashion, called my Drill Sergeant up to him and said, "Give This man enough time to eat." And on he went.

We had not done well on the Sunday inspection, so the cadre sergeant came in later in the week, took us out to the low crawl pits outside the barracks and had the troops doing the low crawl.

Understand, I had that full back brace on and I knew that I had to get to the dispensary.

I wasn't doing the low crawl because, one, it's harassment. It's not part of the training. So, I was standing up against a pine tree about 15 feet away from the entrance to the low crawl pit, and everybody else was doing the low crawl. Finally, the cadre sergeant saw me just standing there.

He came over, "What are you doing?"

I said, "I am just standing here."

"Now, you got to get down. In the pit."

"No. I am not going to do it. I have a bad back."

Then he grabbed me by the lapels of my jacket and shoved me up against that pine tree. I said, "Sergeant, make my day, and tomorrow I will be of equal rank with you."

He slowly let me go. Then he said, "Just lay down in the low crawl pit."

I said, "I can do that."

I laid down in the low crawl pit, and this guy stepped right on my back. This worked right into my plan; I didn't tell a soul. I didn't even tell my friends when I left what I was up to. As far as they were concerned, I had a bad back, and they knew no different. And this guy stepped right on my back in front of the other trainees. The next morning, I used that as an excuse to go to the dispensary, where I got a profile and they took me out of training for a week. A profile is a written medical exemption from certain physical activities and often resulted in light office work in the dispensary. The profile was no stooping, bending, running, jumping, standing over 15 minutes, walking over a quarter mile or carrying anything heavy, such as a weapon.

I had a profile and I was at the dispensary, working. But my drill sergeant scheduled a private meeting with me at 10:00 in the morning in his office, when everybody was out training. In my mind, I knew exactly what that meant. It meant that as soon as I went through that door, they would throw a blanket over my head and beat me to a pulp.

I got up there and his door was just slightly ajar. I launched off the hallway wall behind me and blasted through this door just ready for all hell to break loose and to protect myself, but there was absolutely nobody else in the room. I startled the shit out of the drill sergeant, you know, because I came flying there like Superman, and landed like a maniac in front of him. He gained his composure, slowly looked up from his desk and in a calm voice said, "Cook, why don't you sit down?" Then, with increasing volume, he said, "The reason I called you in here was if everybody knew as much about the Army as you do, we wouldn't need basic training. You don't need to be going and disrupting everything. You know, if you want to protect yourself, it is one thing. You don't have to do it for each platoon, or every guy in your platoon. What they don't know, they don't need to know. And you don't need to educate them."

I said, "Okay. Unless it gets really out of bounds, then, you know, I am going to say something to them."

After the meeting, I went back into the dispensary and I grabbed a whole bunch of double Darvon capsules. If you take the Darvon apart, an aspirin is the powdered form, but inside there is a little double-domed pill. They are pain meds that numb you and I hid them for later use.

A little later, I was issued my Army glasses and I was in the mess hall. Nobody was in there because I worked through lunch at the dispensary and it was late. I was getting something to eat and about, oh, five or six tables down the room, was my supply sergeant. He was looking back at me across these six tables, but I had army issue glasses on, not my dark glasses. So, he was not sure if it was me. There was this kind of stare down for the entire time we were eating lunch. You could tell he was just grinding on it. God, is that him? Is that him?

He finished his lunch, and he said, "Cook, you got a weapon in my supply room that needs to be cleaned."

I said, "Supply Sergeant, I can't clean that weapon because I am not allowed to pick it up. It's against my profile."

He stomped out. The week was going by and we were coming up on the weekend and into Sunday, and Monday I had to start back to basic training again because my profile was expiring. I hadn't yet accomplished my goal of getting to the Tacoma Washington Hospital where my medical discharge was.

Sunday night, I psyched myself up and I actually passed out in formation just prior to dinner. They took me to the dispensary. I don't know how I heated up the thermometer, whether I stuck it on a lamp, rubbed it on my shirt or what. I forgot what I did. But they sent me to the Tacoma Washington Hospital. They thought I had spinal meningitis. I said, "I don't have spinal meningitis. I have a bad back."

They sent me down for X-rays, which I knew they would do.

On the way down to the X-ray, I had a package of gum. I threw the gum away, and I put the tin foil in my mouth and I chewed on it. I got the idea of this from the guys that were swallowing it to show as an ulcer at the Oakland induction center. I figured if I chewed on it and rolled it into a very thin thread, then wrapped it in the label of my underpants; it would look like a crack on the very last vertebrae. I was two years into this planning.

They called my name to get my X-ray, and I went to the bathroom, took this thing out of my mouth, and rolled it into a thread. I wrapped it in the label of my underpants, dead center of my last vertebrae. The X-ray technician said, "Take off your underwear."

Two and a half years of planning was going right out the window. This was my coup de grace I was trying to pull off, and she was going to mess it up. I looked at her and said, "I don't have any metal on me, and I'm not taking my shorts off in front of you."

She said, "Fine. Leave them on." She proceeded to take the X-rays.

The next day, I met with the orthopedic specialist. Accordingly, I took those double-domed pills after removing the aspirin, so that whenever he was poking me, I wouldn't feel it and flinch as bad. I went through his examination and review of my file and then back to my room. A couple days went by and I had another meeting with the orthopedic specialist. In that meeting, he said he was going to recommend me for medical separation from the armed forces. I had a hard time controlling the joy on my face.

Was it the tin foil in my underpants label? Was it the two and a half-inch medical file I had built up over the last couple of years? Or was it the powers that be talking to each other saying, "You know what? This guy does not want to be in the Army. Nor is he a candidate that we want. He is one day from his GI Bill. If we let him out right now, he won't get it."

A few days later, I received medical separation from the Army. So, I was free from the army 3½ weeks from hitting the ground for basic training. But the story was just beginning.

I was medically discharged and out of training, so they put me in the holdover barracks down on the first floor with the permanent party. In addition to that, there were a lot of other guys in the holdover barracks, and the First Sergeant and Drill Sergeant decided there were enough guys in the holdover barracks to pull the KP and all the troops could train. They didn't have to take any of the trainees and put them in the KP. It was also a very good way of getting me back for everything I had done because when you pull KP, you get up at 3:30 in the morning. You report to the kitchen at 4:00. And you work until 9:00 or 9:30 that next night. Now, I pulled KP for like 40-something days straight with the guys in the holdover room.

Then I discovered the guys all had the same profile I had. No stooping, bending, running, jumping, standing over 15 minutes, walking over a quarter mile, or carrying anything heavy, such as a weapon.

I said, "Hey guys. They can't make us do this." I started inciting our profile limitations on the kitchen staff. We had to sit down every 15 minutes so they had us sit down and polish silverware. That was okay. We started saying we were not going to unpack the trucks. The trucks were pulling up behind the mess hall. Normally, KP boys go out and pick up sacks of potatoes and all that kind of stuff. We were not going to do it. Well, they took about a week of this, and the cooks were really getting pissed off. I finally convinced the guys that on Sunday, when the Brigadier General hit the service line, we would walk off the line. The other guys, I mean, they were scared to death.

"You sure you know what you're talking about?"

"Trust me." You know, I was telling the troops all the time, "Trust me." That Sunday morning, at the end of the week, because we were really pushing the cooks, one cook threw all the mops, brooms and stuff out of the storage room and onto the floor, and said, "Cook, pick them up."

I said, "You know, Sergeant, I don't know what wild hair you got up your ass this morning, but you threw them out there, you pick them up."

He got really pissed off, came over and he took a swing at me. I just ducked it, and when it cleared, I hit him with a good right hand, putting him right on the floor. In no time at all, we had the First Sergeant down there. The First Sergeant was a typical, big, large, loudmouthed First Sergeant. He was 6' 2" and I am 5' 8", and he had two guys restraining me because I might hurt him. Really!

An hour and a half went by, and when the General hit the food line and we walked off the line, we walked out the back of the mess hall. We had the cooks, the Captain of the dispensary, the First Sergeant and the Captain, plus some drill sergeants and the General all yelling and screaming at us. The first Sergeant was screaming, "Get your fucking ass back in there."

I said, "You can't make us do this," with coworkers behind me shaking in their boots.

He screamed back, "I can make you do anything!"

They were just down my throat, and I got my line of troops standing behind me saying, "What are they going to do to us?"

I turned to them and said, "Give me your profiles," which I handed over to the General who was quietly standing close by observing. The verbal argument went on while the General reviewed the profiles. I heard the General lean over to the First Sergeant and say, "Wally, he is right. You can't make them do that. You know. No stooping, bending, running, jumping, standing over 15 minutes, walking over a quarter mile, or carrying anything heavy, such as a weapon. You cannot do KP."

That was the end of KP.

My next assignment on that day was to paint the butt cans red, so I went downstairs into the supply room to find the red paint. The Supply Sergeant saw me in there and said, "Cook, what you are doing in my supply room?" as you can guess, I was not his favorite guy.

I said, "Well, I am looking for the red paint. I am supposed to paint the butt cans red." He said, "The paint is in the paint shed outside the building. We do not keep paint in the supply room."

"Well, shit, Supply Sergeant, I didn't know where the paint was."

"What did you say?"

"I said, 'Well, shit, Supply Sergeant, I didn't know where the paint was.'"

"Go see the First Sergeant for an Article 15."

"What for?"

"For saying 'shit' in my supply room."

I went upstairs and I was standing in front of the First Sergeant's door. He had little six by eight windows in it. He saw my pretty little face standing there framed in that little window, and he made me stand out there for another 45 minutes. Every time he looked up, he had to look at my face through that little window. Finally, he called me in and said, "This is the third time in a day that you have been in front of me. Most people don't make that until they have got a year. What is it now? What did you do?"

"Well, I was sent up here to get an Article 15."

"What did you do?"

"I said, 'shit' in the supply room."

"You did what?"

I said the supply sergeant sent me up here to get an Article 15 because I said shit in his supply room.

"Dag nab it. I told you to paint the butt cans red. Now get out of my sight."

I went to get the red paint out of the paint shed, and when I returned, First Sergeant had the Supply Sergeant up against the wall. He just reamed him for sending me up there for that Article 15 for saying "shit" in the supply room.

Periodically, the Captain or First Sergeant would say, "You need a haircut," and I would say, "It's more than a quarter mile, give me a ride and I will get it cut." That did not happen, so my hair was longer than most.

Real close to within a week or so of graduation one night, it was Saturday night, platoon leaders came down to the holdover barracks and woke me up and said, "We're not sure what to do."

I said, "What are you talking about?"

They said, "The Drill Sergeant from 1 and 2 went to 3 and 4. And 3 and 4 went to 1 and 2. They had their own inspection." They just tipped over our footlockers and tipped over our beds and just because things weren't right, they made this huge mess in all four platoons. They did this all the time.

I said, "That's real easy. You have one of two choices. You can do what they want, and that's stay up all night and put this whole thing back together, or you can stand your ground and say you were ready for inspection and this is a result of their inspection." They decided to stand their ground, all four platoons.

Brigadier General went up there to make this inspection, and it looked like a bomb went off in the barracks. He turned around and said to the cadre, "Go get Cook." He sent a guy down to get me, took me into one of the Drill Sergeant's offices, and said, "Do you know what happened here?"

"Yes, sir. I do."

"Well, what happened?"

"They made the choice. They were ready for inspection, and the Drill Sergeants came in here last night and that is the result of their inspection. So, they are just standing their ground in solidarity."

He walked out of that room. He walked right past all the Drill Sergeants, everybody standing in the hallway by the stairway and barracks door and said, "Have a good day, gentlemen. We will see you next week," and went straight out to his car.

My papers finally came in maybe another four or five days, and graduation of the troops was taking place. They didn't let me go when medically discharged; they kept me the whole time.

The Brigadier General personally came and got me in his car to take me to the bus to ship me home. On the way, he stopped by the barbershop and they shaved me bald. Then he took me to the bus station and sent me home.

I used to tell the guys, "You know, call me what you like, but call me at home."

I Call Them Godfather Moments

What is a godfather moment? It is a small action, behavior or sentence that can change the course and direction of life, and most of the times in a negative fashion. In the movie the Godfather when all the heads of the families were meeting and discussing getting into the drug business, the Godfather was having no part in the idea, but his son indicated in his statement that they might consider it. That was a godfather moment that lead to the attempted assassination of the Godfather and resulted in the rest of the story. My brother identified with the movie and its business philosophy. He was secretive and kept his plans close to the chest, like, don't ask me about my business, never let them know what you are thinking. Never trust the competition kind of attitude.

These moments occur all the time, especially in today's politically correct attitude. A statement can ruin your career. They can affect relations with family, friends, and business associates and partners.

Godfather moments can be really damaging and spread out like octopus tentacles or a spider web that affects an unknown amount of people. They happen all the time in today's world. I have experienced these from afar and on a first-hand basis. The affect can domino into 3rd party misrepresentations, misunderstanding and possible loss of relationships and can even result in retaliation as in the Godfather movie.

So be careful what you say or do. Like the old saying Mom used to use, **"If you can't say anything nice, don't say anything at all."**

Life is Not Always Fair

Life is difficult and hard, and seldom does it go as planned. After getting out of the Army, I did what I believed I was supposed to do and that was to get married, start a family and go to work. Although it may seem like I had it all together and under control, I didn't. I was like a duck easily shedding water from my back looking cool and calm, but paddling like mad underneath. Although I didn't know it, I was insecure and immature. I was light in the world and business experience and did not have the full college experience of learning and growth. And Dad wasn't around because of his alcoholism. I was young and had no business being married, but thought that was what I was supposed to do. I wasn't prepared or emotionally mature enough to be married. I hadn't even begun to take care of myself and get into the world, didn't own a TV or a couch, and I got married and took on that load, including a stepdaughter.

Going into business was like when, at 8 years old, my parents signed me up for little league baseball when no one had taught me how to play! I learned as fast as I could from my peers and gave it 110% effort, but still was not very good. The same applied to learning the business. This is where I applied "Listen, listen to the other guy" and educated myself.

I went to work at Dad's office. I needed to produce income, as the company did not have the resources to carry me without producing income. So, I did what I knew how to do and started building houses on lots Dad had in Bowling Green and Parkway Greens, and I also developed a small 10-lot subdivision on the land Dad owned in Northgate. My brother who was five years older had been working in Dad's office completing a couple of small commercial projects but was hampered by Dad's absence due to his alcoholism.

As brothers we were not close, maybe it was the five years between us. I had always thought we would be equal partners, but it didn't happen that way. I don't know why he had to have it all. Was it because of the competitive and winning teachings from Dad to be the best and most successful? Was it the power and control it gave him or was it the Godfather moment when I was about 13-14 and Dad made the statement to my brother that "Tommy is going to pass you up like you're standing still?" Dad knew it was a mistake when he said it, and I do think it had a big impact on my brother in terms of making sure it did not happen or it sure felt that way.

When I was in high school, Dad had formed a corporation called the WITH Corporation; the name was made up from the Wi from William and the Th from Thomas. He gave each of us 10% and distributed the rest of the stock to himself, my mom and grandmother. He never did anything with the corporation, so it had no value. My brother caught dad at a low spot and bought his shares; he then bought all the remaining shares from my grandmother and my mom for pennies, thereby completing the key piece for his strategic plan. Prior to this, he had been working on developing an office building on land that Dad had but could not get the development costs to work due to the construction cost being too high.

Since I had been in construction since 12 and had acquired some architectural education. Because I was taught to listen to the other guy, I was able to cut the construction cost of the project by listening and being educated by the various subcontractors on how to bring the cost down. Then I drew down on the house loans I was building to raise the cash we needed to close the first office building construction loan. The project was successful, but from that point on, it was rob Peter to pay Paul because we used the house money for the commercial project. We had to keep building to stay afloat and successfully did so. Upon completion of this office building, we started a new development and management company called the Cook Company.

While my brother was negotiating my parents' divorce, he negotiated the purchase of Mom's residential properties and non-income producing assets with a note from both of us under the newly formed Cook Company, which was owned by us in a 50-50 partnership. He had structured it to provide steady income from both of us for Mom to live on. At the same time, in order to gain control, he was able to implement his strategic plan wherein he optioned the commercial office land from Mom into the WITH Corporation, making our ownership in the developments a lopsided 90%–10% proposition.

After completing the divorce, and the deal was documented as described above, he waited until we were fishing opening day of trout season to present how things were going to be and the deal that had been made. Although unfair, it was a done deal. Dad was gone and Mom had already agreed. I had nowhere to go. I couldn't back up and work for Mark Ures. Although I didn't burn the bridge, it wasn't something I could return to. I was gung-ho and we had a good salary generated by the management fees collected by the Cook Company, I accepted it. I look back and Dad had always taught me to stand up for myself and I don't know why I didn't. I should have knocked him out on the spot. On the other hand, in hindsight, I'm thankful I didn't. "Be careful what you wish for, you might get it." I could have negotiated, easily. I could have said, "Fuck you, that's not how it's going to be.

I always thought we were going to be equal partners and that's exactly what we're going to be and I'm going to walk out of here and leave you with 10 half-done houses and a half-done office building. And you're not going to have the faintest idea how to recover from it. You better rethink this partnership." Had I stood up for myself, he would have folded. But I didn't. I spent years emotionally struggling and resenting myself for not standing up for myself. Many years passed and I tried to lessen the pain by recognizing that "he didn't fuck me;" "I let him fuck me" because I didn't stand up for myself. Had I just gotten 40% of the shares, it still would have been lopsided; it still would have been controlled by him. Even if it were a 50/50 deal, the success and wealth with the wrong life perception and direction and no balance probably would have killed me.

The unequal ownership was not conducive to a long-lasting partnership. It was unfortunate because we made a really good team together. In the team, I was responsible for the plans and engineering, zoning, cost estimating and construction of the office building shells and tenant improvements. He did the banking, loan packaging and financing, land acquisition and leasing. He was sharp, did a lot of analyzing and strategizing and had impeccable timing with land acquisitions, but the imbalance started wearing on both of us.

We had owned the Cook Co., the management company for the developments, 50/50 but it was just a funneling company and didn't make a big profit. The money and value were in the WITH corporation's ownership of the projects. My partnership with my brother actually cost me more than I received due to paper value upon which deals, taxes and divorces were based but never materialized. Not a penny of cash flow was ever disbursed, but the salaries generated from the Cook Co. management arm were good. Still, we kept building more office projects. Jack Diepenbrock, our business lawyer and, ultimately, my brother's attorney, a pillar of class and the community put us on the map by bringing us a joint venture partner from Mainline Corporation of Australia with an infusion of capital for more land acquisitions.

We needed this, as we were running out of our developable land required to continue building and pay off "Peter." But shortly after the joint venture had purchased new land holdings, the company went into receivership. This could have been really problematic, but my bother quickly negotiated the deal wherein they left the capital invested on the table rather than be sued by us, their partner. So, it was a quick divorce and a win–win for us.

My brother kept everything secretive and at times, he was paranoid about financial crises and the possible collapse of the economy. During the time of the oil crises, he wanted to have a place that was removed but self-sufficient in the event of a financial collapse. He wanted me to investigate and find such a property. One day in passing, he asked if I had done any investigating and I lied and said, "Yes, in fact I bought a place and if there is ever a collapse, you and your family are more than welcome." Then I said, "There is only one thing. You only get 10% of the food and water." It was another godfather moment that really put a strain on the relationship and from that point on, he could not look me in the face.

Brochure Picture for My New Company

The strain forced me to start my own construction company, and I still built all of our WITH Corporation projects for the next five years from a separate office where we did not have to interact on a daily basis. Our relationship came to an end when we had completed the development of the WITH Corporation land holdings. By this time, my drinking and alcoholism were progressing and I was just about to get much worse when I started using cocaine. He did not want to be associated with me at that time and rightfully so, despite the fact that a few years later, I had stopped drinking and doing cocaine. But still we were estranged for the next 15 years.

EXPENSIVE BLAZE

One night, I was down at Fanny Ann's in Old Sacramento drinking with some friends who had to leave at closing time. I wasn't done partying so I called my friend Jack Giere who lived down off Florin Road. He said, "Come on over." I closed down Fanny Ann's and headed out I-5 towards his house. I wasn't really paying attention and I missed the florin road exit, which meant I had to drive all the way out to Twin Cities Road, seven and a half miles out of my way, because I-5 was not yet completed. I drove all the way out to Twin Cities Road and made the U-turn to head back into town. It was just open freeway with nobody on it, so I thought, well let's see how fast this new Porsche will go.

I took it up to about 135 and I was just screaming down the freeway. All of a sudden, my engine quit and I looked down at my gauges trying to find out what the hell was going on. I looked up in the rearview mirror and the whole back end of the car was on fire! What happened, I guess, was there was a little hole or something in the fuel line that they didn't detect or that opened up. So, I started getting onto the brakes and into the gears to get the thing stopped. At that point, a sheriff going south, while I was going north, went by me and I was still going, at that point, 80 miles an hour or so. I must have looked like a rocket going by him.

I got the car stopped on the side of the freeway. I happened to have a tennis shirt hanging in the back of my car, so I grabbed that shirt and popped the rear hood and tried to put the fire out with the shirt. I tried to muff it out. That wasn't working. Well, I'd been drinking all night, so what I did was I pissed on it. That put it out, with the exception of one little flame, but I had forgotten to turn off the key, so the fuel pump was still, ph, ph, ph, and it went right back up.

By this time, the sheriff was there on the other side of the road and I ran across to him and said, "Give me your fire extinguisher." He wouldn't give it to me because he thought it was going to blow up. I said, "The gas tank's in the front of the car. Let me use the fire extinguisher." He said, "No, it's going to blow up." I didn't want to argue with him because I had been drinking. I had to sit there on the side of the road and watch my Porsche burn to the ground. As I was watching, the news crew showed up and it ended up in the morning paper under the heading "EXPENSIVE BLAZE."

The Sierra Trek

It was 1977, and I was 30 and newly divorced when my friend Steve Crowle invited me to go on the Sierra trek with him and 25 other people. This was 110-mile trek from Kennedy Meadows to the floor of Yosemite Valley. I had not done much back packing in the previous 10 years other than a couple of short trips. I was free to be able to go on this adventure and off we went. This was at the beginning of life in the fast lane for both Steve and me and other friends. That lasted another four years.

Like the Eagle' song, "We were running down that freeway, messed around and got lost; we didn't care, we were just trying to get off." Steve and I took a quarter ounce of cocaine with us to begin the trip and stayed up to the wee hours of the morning talking and singing. I was trying to teach him the words to James Taylor's song "Sweet Baby James." We had to get up early and trek another 11 miles up and over Brown Bear Pass into the emigrant wilderness, which resembled a moonscape, then over Bond Pass and into beautiful Yosemite to Grace Meadows. It is amazing that no matter what direction you hike into Yosemite, when you cross the boundary line, you know you are in Yosemite.

It was the third week in July, and it had been a heavy snow year, meaning there was snow crossing at the peaks and raging high water crossing. The crossing at Stubblefield was slow moving, but neck deep in freezing cold water. The next day in Kerrick Canyon, the crossing was roaring rapids and we had a rope across the river and a human chain to guide people across without being swept downstream.

As people were making it across, a baby fawn went floating by. My friend Mike Nolasco broke rank and went running downstream and caught up with the baby deer, pulled it from the water where we wrapped it up to regain its body heat, then we released it to anxious mommy deer that had been pacing above us on the hillside. We continued on that day to Benson Lake, which later became a special spot for me for the next 35 years. We still had another 60 miles left to the valley.

From Benson, we hiked to Matterhorn Canyon then on through Glen Aulin to our restock in Tuolumne and then trekked on to Cathedral Peaks where someone had a couple jars of white lightning moon shine. I started making cowboy coffee keyokies: coffee, Swiss Miss and moon shine. We fired up the entire camp of 25. The kids had a big bonfire and people were howling at the moon, so to speak. Everyone was shitfaced. From there, it was the last day's hike into the valley stopping at Half Dome on the way down. Out of the 25 people on the trip, the two least likely guys to get together for the next 35 years were me and my friend Dave Gustafson, but that is the friendship that developed because of the trek and our mutual love for backpacking and the yearly trips we did together into Benson Lake.

The Sierra trek, what a trip! Although I did know it at the time, it was to have a huge impact on my life moving forward. Not only did it tone my body, but it opened up the mountains, nature, passion for backpacking, and my friend Dave. More importantly, it brought to the surface my buried interest of wanting to know and learn how our ancestors lived and survived, their knowledge and skills.

Because of that, I started backpacking again and wanted to learn about the edible plants to have fresh food on the trail. The plants led to the sticks and the sticks led to the rocks and I wanted to know how to make fire with sticks, how to make cordage, traps and triggers, tan a hide, flint nap a point, make a bow and arrows, baskets and pottery, etc. Once I got started, for years I was trying to learn this stuff out of a book thinking I was the only nut in the world interested in this knowledge and skills. Ever try riding a bike out of a book?

With four years of living in the fast lane, I had struggled to stay sober over a number of years and stayed dry for only 80-90 days on several occasions. I thought I could find an easier, softer way but could not, until it finally took. But in my struggles and new reality, somehow my interest automatically lead me to nature and wanting to know the skills as I did on my first backpacking trip at 12 years old. Maybe in a past life, I was an early 1800s mountain man? I needed to get back to the ground and start building from there. All the people around me wondered what I was doing, but as good friends do, they just let me pursue this new interest.

Quip: It's never quite as good or quite as bad as you really think it is.

This one came up later in another one of our evening talks. Dad had seen me at high points and low points and I am not sure whether the conversation occurred because of a great deal that caused jubilation, some major business problem or a costly event loss. His point was, temper your emotions; it's great that you were successful in making this profitable deal and that's good, but it is not the whole picture. They're not always going to be that way. On the other hand, you may have lost this great deal and feel that without it, things are just falling apart and a doomsday feeling is upon you. In reality, it is not as bad as you think it is. The world keeps turning and you will survive because it's not as bad as you think it is. Don't take yourself so seriously!

Out of everything bad comes something good.

Proper Way to Throw a Punch

When I was a very young boy, my dad spent quite a bit of time with me in the living room teaching me how to properly throw a punch. He went over the correct way to spin my wrist at the very last moment, how to properly launch off my big toe because that is where your best right hand comes from. He taught me a whole lot about sliding forward and backward, bobbing and weaving, and properly throwing a punch.

When I went to St. Robert School, I walked by Joaquin Miller and Hollywood Park schools on my way. While walking down the sidewalk, this kid came at me. He stopped and said, "My name is Mike Thomason, and I am the baddest kid in Hollywood Park." I said, "Well, good for you and have a good day." I started to move. He said, "No, no, no. You don't understand. I am the baddest kid in school, and you can't pass."

At that point, we were standing about two arm lengths between us and out of each other's range, but I could tell a fight was about to happen. As he was telling me I could not pass, I had moved my right foot in behind my left foot without moving my upper body, giving the appearance that there was still space between us. I said, "Excuse me." Then I launched off my big right toe, covered the space between us with elusive speed, let that right hand go and dropped him. Boom! It was the first time I ever tried it, and it worked really well. I hit him on the cheekbone and just put him down, blackened his eye. I walked around him and said, "You have a good day." No, he wasn't so bad after that.

There were other times. I never picked a fight, but there were three or four times when it came my way and that right hand came in and ended it right there. Boom! On the ground, lights out. So, the proper way of throwing a punch results in a lot of energy that you can deliver.

After I returned from the 100-mile Sierra trip when I found Benson Lake, every ounce of me was just solid. When I left for the trek, I weighed 154 pounds. I lost four pounds on the trek but then dropped to 140 pounds, and my body transformed itself. Even though I only weighed 140 pounds, I had been going down to the Y once a week boxing with my friend Frank Schetter and Mike Hjelmeland, just working out on the heavy bag. We did a little sparring, but it was really just a workout. If we did spar there were two rules: you only hit as hard as you want to be hit back and we both have to go to work tomorrow.

Frank was a much better boxer than I was and we squared off to spar a little. Well, I have a pretty quick left jab, but every time I threw it, Frank's left jab would smack me in the face. I knew I was telegraphing it somehow, but could not figure it out. I said "Frank, what am I doing wrong?" He said, "You figure it out." But his left kept hitting me in the face and after 3 rounds, I said, "Come on, Frank, what am I doing wrong?" He said, "You are pumping your left two times before you throw it!" We came out for round 4 and I pumped my left twice but did not throw it and slid my head to the right as his left jab missed and then came over the top with a right cross. Frank said, "I knew I shouldn't have told you."

Some two years later, my dad was sitting across my desk from me in the office, and we were having a conversation. A framing contractor showed up at my office door because I owed him $30,000, but I wasn't paying him because the carpenter's union had filed a $30,000 lien against the project, claiming the framing contractor had used off-site non-union labor for the job. Until it was cleared, I was not going to pay him, obviously.

The subcontractor was in there hassling with my controller, then he came to my doorway and I said, "Charlie, get the union lien taken care of and I will pay you tomorrow." With that, he started yelling profanities and what have you, and I said, "Charlie, the conversation is over. Just have your attorney contact mine."

SERMONS FROM THE GREEN LEATHER CHAIR

He left my doorway, walked over to my secretary's desk and cleared the desk of everything on it, typewriter in those days and the calculator, all that stuff, onto the floor. I walked out of the office and I said, "Charlie, time for you to leave. I was fairly calm. He walked between the double doors, into the reception room, picked up the lamp between the two wing chairs, and threw it at me. I blocked it with my hand as it fell on the floor and shattered.

He was calling me out saying, "I'm going to kick your ass." I stepped over the lamp and I said, "Charlie, it's time for you to leave." Now, this guy was a framing contractor. He was probably 6'1", probably 220 pounds. I mean a big boy. He backed up to the reception room desk, and at about that point, my dad came out between those double doors and yelled at him, "You asshole, get out of here!" at about a volume 10. This guy picked up the three-hole punch, not one of those little ones, I'm talking about the five pounder with the big bar; he threw it clear across the reception room and hit my dad in the shoulder. Almost hit him in the head with it.

I said, "That's it." And I went after this guy; my intention was just to get him out the door. As I approached and got into striking range, way too quickly, he was throwing this roundhouse right at me from the ground. I am there way too early. I mean, his arm is still way out here and coming. I brought my two fists up to get them into fighting position, real slow, and I knew my eyes got really big. I got up on my tiptoes to get myself even a little bit higher. Then at the last second, I just dropped straight down and his right hand went straight over my head brushing my hair.

He was all wrapped up with this right arm across his body and his chin sticking straight out there. I hit him with a straight left hand right on the button. Boom! I knock him back into the wall.

I went after him and he threw a left jab, which I slipped as it went by my head and over my left shoulder. I came right over the top of that, with a right cross and he ducked his head. I caught him with my baby knuckle in the forehead and I cut him open on his forehead, which ripped my whole knuckle out and split my hand. Then he threw a right at me and I bobbed down, as his punch came right over the top of my head again. I hooked him to his right cheek with a left hook.

I knew that after that, he was wide open up the middle and then here came that right hand. I could hear my dad in the back go, "Ooh," when I hit him with that right hand. So, then it was another left hook to the top of the temple, and another right on the center of his nose. Then another left to the right to his jaw. At the same time, there was this voice I could hear and this scratching at my back. This voice was starting to come through. Then I hit him again with a right and the voice was saying, "You're going to kill him. You're going to kill him." I backed off and he looked just like a tree, just falling, straight on his face. After coming to, he crawled out the door and we locked it. I guess he was out on his feet because as far as I was concerned, he was still standing in front of me until my dad pulled me off.

We called the police and described the events. My hands were just the biggest mess, swollen bruises and cuts and possibly broken. The guy threw four punches at me and missed me with every one of them. I threw eight punches at him and hit him on the button with all of them. We waited around for about an hour and the police still hadn't shown up. I said, "You guys stay here. I'm going to the emergency room to get my hands x-rayed." I wanted to see if there was anything broken. I went to the emergency room and the police came to the office where they found a loaded .38 in the man's camera case with hollow point bullets in it. He had left a clipboard and his camera case when he crawled out the door. The guy came back when the police were there, trying to get them to arrest me for beating the shit out of him.

And they said, "Well, not tonight, pal. You're going to jail for carrying a weapon." They also took him to whatever emergency room and stitched him up big time. Then they sent a policeman over to get my statement over at the emergency room. While I was sitting in the hallway, the policeman came through the door and walked right by me. He went down to the orderly station and said "I'm looking for the guy that was in a fight."

The orderly guy pointed to me. I could see the sheriff shake his head, no, no, no, and I could see the orderly shaking his head, yes, yes, yes. That's him. He walked back down the hallway and looked at me and said, "Would you stand up for me?" I stood up and he said, "Damn, you don't look big enough to do that kind of damage."

My dad had taught me how to properly throw a punch. After some time had passed, I was out to lunch and I tried to talk to him about that night, but my dad changed the subject and would not talk about that fight because he thought I was going to kill the man and it scared him. He had never seen me in a fight and what he taught me scared him. That's the reason he never talked to me about it. He did not want to promote it in any way. But after he passed, I talked to a one of his friends. I said, "Did my dad ever tell you about the fight I got into?" He said, "Absolutely, he told me. He thought you were going to kill him."

Actually, I was lucky to pick up his round house right and duck under it, which set up the whole series of punches that followed. It also didn't hurt that I had been at the gym boxing and working out on the heavy bag.

Quip: WORK, WORK, WORK (REVISITED)

From time to time, my dad would walk into my office and quote one of his quips or other information he wanted to pass on and then walk out.

One day he came into my office and said, "You know how I taught you that you work, work, work even though you don't feel good?" I said, "I know it well." He said, "Well I am here to tell you that I was wrong. If you're sick, go home. It does not do anyone any good." And out the door he went.

New Porsche

This Porsche was my third Porsche. I had burned the first one up in the expensive blaze and later bought another one that I later traded for a brand new 911SC. We were building the Tavern Inn Condominiums in Squaw Valley. I was headed back to Sacramento after the meeting and heading up Donner Pass out of Truckee when a 380Z started playing with me; you know, let's race up the hill.

I was driving my new Porsche 911SC, so I just took it up to a little over 100 miles an hour going up the grade and over the summit and blew the doors off the "Z". After cresting the summit, I kept driving at over 100 mph all the way down the mountain until I was leading into Lincoln/Roseville just above Sacramento. This section of Interstate 80 is a straight five miles of a six-lane rolling mountain super slide that you can see from top to bottom. While crowning the last hump at the bottom, I could see the red light at the top of the hill in my rear-view mirror. I pulled the car over, got out, walked around to the passenger side, got my registration, insurance, my wallet, and my license out, and stood there waiting for him on the shoulder.

A few minutes later, he pulled up. He got out of the car and leaned on his door; he had this kind of smirk smile on his face. He said, "New Porsche, huh?" I said, "Yes, sir." He walked around to me and said, "Driver's license, registration, insurance." I had them at the ready. He said, "Tell me, how fast you were going?"

"Well, when I saw your light at the top of the hill, I was going 103."

"Uh-huh. How long have you been doing that?

"Do you want me to lie to you or do you want me to tell you the truth?"

"Tell me whatever you want."

"Would you believe since Truckee?"

"Yeah, you know that 380Z that was trying to catch you? My partner picked him off because neither one of them could catch you. I have been chasing you for 49 miles. I've been going 120 in the straights, 85 in a four-wheel slide, and you're out here for a fucking Sunday drive in excess of 110 miles an hour."

"YES, SIR."

"Do you suppose you got the carbon burned out on this new machine?"

"Oh, yes, sir."

"Why did you stop? Did you run out of gas?

"No SIR, but I knew the red light wasn't for anybody but me, and that is why I stopped."

He wrote me a ticket for 95 in a 65 and let me go.

I think he really enjoyed the ride and chase, plus as I was taught, I treated him with the respect that he deserved and I did not lie to him. By doing so, he gave me a break.

At the time, I thought this was pretty cool and that I was pretty hot shit. But looking back, I was anything but. I was an out-of-control cocky little shit, "Mr. Hip, Slick and Cool" pushing the limits of everything, almost like an unconscious death wish. Or just so arrogant that I was invincible and none of it in line with Dad's teachings of class and behavior. Somehow my guardian angel has been with me my entire life.

Struggles and Survival

Looking back, I was probably an alcoholic from the age of 12 when Russell Daniel and I drank almost a fifth of Cuttysark one night; I just would not admit it until I was about 34. Dad had gained his sobriety years earlier and was in my office daily. He patiently watched me. I was about 34 when we went to San Francisco to meet with a banker on a deal Dad was working on. We met at the bank, then went to lunch where I had a drink and the banker had three drinks. After we concluded our meeting, Dad and I were walking back to the car when I said, "Hey Dad, why did that guy have so many drinks? Was he trying to get high?"

My dad looked at me and said, "High? "He is trying to get well." We walked a little further and I was beginning to realize alcohol could be a problem for me.

So I asked my dad, "Where is the line?"

He said, "Well, it's in a different place for different people."

I said, "That doesn't tell me much."

He turned to me and with his angry face and tone he said, "That may not tell you anything but you will know when you cross it."

As the years went by and my alcoholism got worse, he would catch me at a low point to try to get my attention and get me to look at the problem. From time to time, he would mention these quips.

"There a seat in AA that's reserved for you.

"It's a down elevator and you can get off at any floor you want."

"Poverty is not a prerequisite of the program but it certainly helps."

"Nobody cares what's in your glass."

Take care of yourself and you will take care of everyone else."

"Not yet!"

And many more.

Still the years rolled by and things got worse with the combination of cocaine and alcohol. It was life in the fast lane "blowing and burning, blinded by thirst and didn't see the stop sign and took a turn for the worst" (Don Henley, Eagles). She is very seductive and will suck you in and spit you out, just like the song says "if you want to get down, down on the ground cocaine." It was before they had GPS. My car was equipped with auto drive to the drug store, amazing. It would automatically drive there!!

It took me another three plus years to finally stop drinking and doing cocaine. First, I went to the care unit, then two times to Duffy's in Calistoga. Gene Duffy was alive at the time and was a great speaker who composed alcoholic stories that hit home. Thank God they videotaped them so they can be used to help practicing alcoholics at Duffy's today. One of my favorites was a tape that we listened to in the front room. I am not sure of the actual title but I call it "Mr. Hip, Slick and Cool."

Gene's story was eloquent as he described Mr. Hip, Slick and Cool, done in such a way that it fit everyone from the banker/lawyer to the janitor. He built you and the story up as to the things you accomplished, the deals you made, the cars you drove, and how good you are. Why! You're Mr. Hip, Slick and Cool, you are a really important and powerful person. Then at the end, in essence, he said you are so hip, slick and cool that your best efforts got you here to my facility. The best that you could do got you here! It hit home. I loved the saying, "You're here as a result of your best efforts" and it has become one of my own quips.

Even though I went to these rehab facilities, they helped but did not take. I struggled in earnest for several years while going to AA. I would get 75-80 days and then just short of 90 days, I would go out and get drunk! Amazingly, every time I did that and came out of the bar, there was a full moon!! It was the 4th of July and I got drunk again. After sobering up, I gained enough guts to go back to my meeting and let them know that once again I had failed. In that meeting, one of the old timers said he would never drink again for the rest of his life. When it was my turn to speak, I said, "I don't know why I keep failing, I guess I am just stubborn." Then I said, "And I don't know how you (referring to the 25-year member) can say you will never drink again."

He said, "In these meetings, we don't talk out of turn, but in this case, I must make an exception because you were not listening. What I said was I will never successfully have another drink for the rest of my life. I can go out this afternoon and have a drink but it won't be successful." Then the conversation moved around the room to another 25+ year member who said "Cook, you're not stubborn—you're stupid." I left that meeting angry and pissed off. But it somehow got my attention and as simple as it is, the fact that it just won't be successful was clear to me and I haven't had a drink since. That was 38 years ago.

Because it won't be successful.

My Friend Steve Crowle

I met Steve in kindergarten at Holy Spirt but then I went to Sutterville school for second and third grades. We were reunited in the fourth grade at St. Robert school and became life-long friends. Steve was the one who went backpacking with me into desolation when we were 12 and backpacked with me through the years. He was the one who invited me to go on the Sierra trek that opened up the mountains and led to my passion for the skills, resulting in a change in life perspective.

He was a tough one; he was intense and sometimes an angry young man who struggled with life. I was one of the few people who could calm him down and whom he would listen to. He was a fighter and tough as nails. I know, because we got into three fights and he kicked my ass twice. But in the second fight, I hit him with the right hand that dad taught me how to throw and knocked him to the ground, which was a rare occurrence, as he could really take a punch. I could have pounced on him but didn't, knowing he would probably whoop me anyway. I stuck out a flat hand as he was getting up from the floor and said, "That's enough, we don't need to take this further." We walked out of there arms around each other and buddies that we were.

He was with me at Benson Lake during the air drop and made the trip into Benson for many years. We went through the cocaine and alcohol period and I later helped him get sober, but he had numerous back surgeries and the prescription drugs took their toll. Then he got cancer and died from it.

Before his death, he made me promise to take his ashes to Benson Lake, which I did. I let his ashes sit in camp for most of the week while I decided where to bury them. There was a small tree just outside of the camp whose roots were exposed due to the beach being washed out from under it. It looked like it was struggling and that fit Steve. So, I decided to do it on Thursday evening. After breakfast, someone put the frying pan under the roll table, and the strap was hanging down.

As the Benson winds started in the morning, the strap would swing up and out then come back and hit the fry pan—"DING"–"DING" then pause and do it again "DING"–"DING" like a church bell. I let it chime all day and then went out to dig the hole at the struggling tree. When I did there was a circle marked out in the sand from the base of that tree where I had planned on burying my friend. I went back into camp and asked who made the circle outside of camp. Juanita's nephew Michael said he did. I asked him to tell me about it. He said it was a life circle and everything inside was good to keep the bad outside from coming in. I said that was perfect and we had a small ceremony in Steve's honor. When we finished, the wind had died down and the chimes stopped DINGING. Actually, pretty amazing. But there are no accidents.

Benson Lake Revisited

It was 1984 when we did the air drop and first trip to Benson Lake, and it became a special place and joy in life. Benson Lake trips became almost a yearly thing over the past 35 years, mostly because of the beauty of it. We typically stayed on the beach for 7 to 10 days eating gourmet food with a big group of people and having a great time. You cannot go on this trip and not have it imprinted on your mind for the rest of your life. We've taken 9- and 10-year-olds and walked them over 45 miles; they can't wait to go back. There are a lot of life lessons in nature, backpacking, and survival skills. Nature is one of those teachers; she will educate you if you don't do the things that are needed and there is nobody to blame. The stories I could tell of people and events that occurred over the last 30 years during these trips. I could write another book.

Benson Lake is so far out in Yosemite that backpackers are typically just passing through after maybe scheduling a layover day or two in their trips. Many come in late afternoon, layover the next day and then get up and out the next morning. Many times when we arrive, there are people camping in our fire and kitchen area! Not a problem. I just bribe them with chicken fajitas, Caesar salad, French bread and wine for dinner if they will move their tent 20 feet.

One year, we arrived before the pack station crew and started setting up camp. We set up the framework for the wind break, built the fire pit, found my buried two-foot square, steel metal hot plate for the fire, started the wood pile and installed the shelves in the kitchen tree in preparation for the arrival of the packers and mules.

Coffee Cake and Roasted Turkey at Benson Lake

The year before, I had stashed some of our pots and a Coleman stove. When I went to retrieve them, they had been dug up from between the two logs I used to bury them and were scattered on the ground nearby. One of the large pots had a hole punched in the top rim where the bear's claw went through it. The stove had been opened and thrown about, breaking the fuel line. We had no stove! Everyone said, "what are we going to do now?" I said, "We will cook in the fire." Then I said, "I am going to the store. I will be back." and walked out of camp.

Some twenty minutes later, I returned to camp with a brand, new Coleman stove! "Where did you get that?" they asked. "At the store!" I told them. "No really, where did you get the stove?" I said, "I made a deal with the people down the beach who were leaving and they had a stove."

On another trip, there were two ladies who were camping 100 feet down the beach enjoying their layover day. I think their names were Kathy and Ellen. We invited them over for wine and desert after we got camp set up. The packers and 10 mules showed up late in the day as the ladies were having their dinner watching our camp.

The pack bags started dropping to the ground and people were grabbing the bags and distributing the contents of each bag. Everyone was working without talking to each other, and everything was set up in minutes. The wind break tarp went onto the premade frame, bear boxes under the lean-to tarp, kitchen table and equipment to the kitchen area, kitchen shelves stocked, chairs all set up, ax and saw shovel in the tool area, wash table station with fishing and tackle area on the lake side of the kitchen tree. The entire camp was set up within 10 minutes. Kathy and Ellen came over after it was done and were astonished at how fast camp came together in such an orderly fashion without anyone talking to each other. I said that is because everyone has been here before and knows where everything goes. They stayed for wine and the Air Drop and a few other Benson stories. It was a great time around the fire. They were sorry they did not have another layover day in their plan.

Another year, we convinced our friend Ken Bell who was not a backpacker to go on the Benson trip. Nobody had given any thought to the fact that Ken had never been packing before. I had given him the shopping list for the meat portion of the trip. The long and short of it is he went to Costco and bought more than the list, thinking the kids would eat it. Ken showed up for the trip with a suitcase and a car camping sleeping bag wearing leather Lederhosen.

He did have a backpack, but it barely held the sleeping bag. This is a 22-mile hike and leather Lederhosen rubbed the skin off his legs after the first day. We had to duct tape his legs to stop the chafing. After we arrived at Benson and unpacked, I realized we had way too much chicken and other meats and not enough coolers. To solve that problem, we invited everyone on the beach to dinner for the next three nights just to get rid of the extra food. On the third night, Ken had a fair amount of wine along with our invited guests when we realized that after three nights of guests, the wine boxes were emptying quickly. To prevent further wine loss, Ken threw a blanket over the boxes and sat down on them to guard the remainder. Meanwhile, he got all he wanted. He got more pie-eyed and funny providing evening entertainment that was fun to watch.

In 1993, I had talked my best friend Chris to go with me into Benson. Not a backpacker, so he rode in on a horse. On the long 22-mile ride in, he developed a severe case of bursitis in his hip that left him somewhat immobile for the entire week and was not getting any better. How were we going to get him out when he can't walk and can't ride a horse? We sent Dave Gustafson, "rocket man," out days early to get help.

As the week ended and the packers and mules arrived to take us out, we had no idea if Dave was successful or not in getting help. The plan was that I would stay with Chris until help arrived as everyone was packing up to start hiking back out. Then we heard the helicopter coming through the gap to the south and landing on the far west side of the beach. We carried Chris to the copter and off he went. Ten minutes later, he was in Tuolumne Meadows. They called his wife Debbie to come get him in Tuolumne with no explanation of what was wrong and why he been flown to the Meadows. It was a frantic trip to a place three hours away that she had never been to before. But she was relieved to find out that he was fine, just could not walk. After getting home, Chris went to the doctor who said it was bursitis and he needed to walk!!

On the trip to bury Steve Crowle, Jaunita's nephew Michael had a 14", two-and-a-half-pound Bowie knife that he whipped out, comparing it to my 3" little Mora knife saying, "That's not a knife, this is a knife." I said, "My little knife will outdo your knife 100 times over. The only thing that knife is useful for is chopping." He argued with me and I said, "OK, lets make a fire board, bow and spindle." Mine was done in minutes and he hadn't even gotten started. It's too big to whittle ends, too cumbersome to cut notches, and actually too big for splitting off the fire board.

Just the other day, my friend Wayne Herman received a text from his grandson Ben whom he had taken on one of the Benson Lake trips many years ago. The text read, "Is Tom going to do another Benson trip as my boys are the same age as I was and I want them to experience the best trip I have ever taken." That sure made me feel good. Benson lake a special place full of memories.

If you go on this trip it will return in your mind year after year as if it was yesterday.

Slow Road

As simple as it was, "it won't be successful" got me to finally stop and begin my slow road to a new and better life. Originally, because of Dad's teachings, I wanted to be worth many millions by the time I was 40. Well, just like Dr. Seuss said in Oh! The Places You Will Go, then you didn't! During my recovery, my interest in learning the edible plants for backpacking that years later led to the passion for learning primitive skills started to give me a new and different perspective on life and living that slowly developed over time. In the first stages of recovery, I was lost in a new reality, "fake it till you make it," and I didn't really know where I was going, but time has a way of showing you the path.

In the beginning, my second wife Linda and I were still living the high life, living in an upscale neighborhood known as the Fabulous 40s, driving expensive cars and spending money we didn't have. The load was beginning to be too much, and I became unwilling to carry it. Additionally, I had changed the marriage contract and was no longer interested in life in the fast lane. So, we sold the big house and separated. But years later, we got back together again when I broke my back skiing in Aspen.

Broken Back

In 1989, I broke my back skiing in Aspen and got back together with my second wife Linda. After a short while, we were back living in the fabulous 40s with a new Mercedes and all the material wants. Then through the years with an economic downturn, the cash flow problems were straining me, the business and our marriage again. In the business, our bonding capacity diminished, making it harder to get the amount of work we needed to break even. I was tired of buying shit we didn't need with money I did not have to impress people I did not know or care about. One time, I was complaining about my wife's continued spending and purchasing of things she didn't need and she said, "Well, you always seem to be able to get funds into my account." I said, "Did it ever occur to you that it is someone else's money?" I was not happy with the stress and strain needed to carry this load and life style and I needed to fix it, but still it took years to finally make the decision to leave and start anew.

CALL OF THE WILD

In the wilderness you are free. I like to take high-powered professional people who think they are in complete control of their world and environment into Benson Lake where they are not in control or have power over anything except their backpack. Under these conditions, they can be fun to watch. That's because they are uncomfortable not being in control. I might not know where I am, but I am not lost – and it's comforting knowing that this is the case.

The Sierra Trek eventually blossomed into my interest in primitive skills. I had done the typical backpacking where you pack in 6-8 miles then base camp and hike around, but the Sierra trek opened up the Sierras to me along with the high country of Yosemite and the discovery of Benson Lake. This was the beginning of the slow change in the right direction and further changes that occurred because of it. Not only did it return me to nature but tied directly into my interest in the woodman's knowledge and skills.

After many years of trying to teach myself the skills, a fantastic basket maker and teacher named Peg M., and now friend of 34 years, came to town to do a hand drill fire-making class using sticks, and she brought a road-kill deer. I was in heaven; she changed my life and opened the door to my interest. I got my fire and got to process a deer. She then tapped me into other people who taught various classes in primitive skills at the "old ways" seminars above Santa Cruz in Henry Cowell Park.

After a couple of years doing these weekend skills classes, in 1992 I went on to BOSS (Boulder Outdoor Survival School) for a 14-day walk-about in the Escalante Drainage near Boulder Utah. Fourteen days of surviving in the Utah red rock country. What an experience. I had a great time, learned a lot, and made lifetime friends with my instructors. David Holladay, Rob Withrow and Carrie Ryan.

David Holladay was one of our guides. He is a desert man—holy man. Throughout the trip, I was overly impressed with the man that he was and I still am. Towards the end of the trip, after our three-day solo, they gave us a map and said you are here and we want you in this other location 16 miles cross-country by tomorrow at 6:00 pm. The group decided to sleep then get up really early rather than start that late afternoon and walking till dark in order to make it to our destination. As the sun was setting and we were under a large cave overhang, we started to drift off to sleep when David Holladay started singing Robert Service's poem "The Call of the Wild is Calling You" to his own music and tempo.

It was beautiful and the words resonated with me because that was exactly what was happening to me. The wild was calling me. Since then and every year, I have always asked David to sing it for me. I like for other people to hear it, but many times in his humbleness, he will take me to the side and sing it only for me without knowing how important it was and has been to me for all these years.

I met Dave Wescott on my first 14-day walkabout with BOSS when he owned it; I loved experiencing that trip and I learned many basic skills. I was impressed that he met us at 3:00 am after our two-week adventure and before we made the last trek to town in the dark.

After that trip, thinking about David Holladay, I was not sure if I had been in the presence of Jesus Christ. His spirit was warm and enlightening. But through the years, even though he kind of looks like Jesus, he is just a special spiritual person that is a friend of 30 years. I had kept that belief to myself until one day many years later, at Winter Count I was talking with both Dave Wescott and Dave Holladay and I said to Holladay when I finished my walkabout, I thought you were Jesus Christ and Dave Wescott said, "So did he." He may not be Jesus but he has a social presence and I am still learning from him.

Dave Holladay

Immediately after the walkabout, when I arrived home, I took my backpack down and took everything out. They called me parts man; if you needed it, I was probably carrying it. Well, that changed dramatically. I realized I didn't need to carry all that stuff and weight because I didn't need it.

Then I jumped on a plane, flew to Salt Lake and went to my first Rabbitstick rendezvous in Rexburg, Idaho, which Dave restarted in 1988. This is a gathering of teachers and instructors in all of the various outdoor bush craft disciplines and skills and you can learn anything you want to learn at the gathering. Dave permeates the entire event. He's a decisive leader. Great man who inspires and motivates me. I am fortunate to know and spend time around him. Actions say more than words.

David and his Rabbitstick were a big part of my continued sobriety and opened up the whole world of people and their lives and teachings, who, over the years, have become a family of friends that has changed my perspective and life. I am not alone in this experience, many if not all are positively affected by the community and humanity that happened as a result of Dave Wescott. I have a tremendous respect and admiration for all that he is and has done. "Class, you know it when you see it."

At the Rabbitstick gathering, there is so much to be learned that it will take you years to make or participate in all the skills and classes that are offered. I was a gung ho student for the first 13 years, but I always brought some wild duck to cook and share at the fire. Then with Dave Westcott's approval, I morphed into the duck man at these primitive skills events. Dave Westcott, along with a man named Larry Dean Olson, started and promoted the primitive skills movement that has now blossomed nationwide.

My survival studies and the family of people helped me tremendously in my own life struggles and survival. Although I go from buckskins to a tux and enjoy everything in between, I love being in the dirt sitting around a fire in my buckskins with a bunch of friends. It has given me a much better perspective on life and on what is important.

Life is like backpacking; the difference between needs and wants in a survival situation is very clear, I need shelter, fire and water. In life, it is not that clear. Do you really need those new shoes? How much weight are you willing to carry? The same is true with life. That new car or big house you just bought puts a lot of weight in your pack; hope there are no steep mountains in front of you.

These teachings, the people and experiences slowly over the many years seeped into my life, making clear the difference between needs and wants and what's really important. At one point, I wanted it all and worked hard in that endeavor. But that started to change slowly and maybe began when I was driving back to work after a great duck hunt and sunrise on a Wednesday morning with me and my dog.

I was feeling guilty for not being at work because Dad always said you work, work, work even if you're not feeling well. Then my brain said, "Hey wait a minute, didn't you just have a great morning? YES! Well, pal, from this point forward you, you are not going to work on Wednesdays." When I got back to the office, I announced that during duck season, I was not going to be in the office on Wednesdays, unless of course it was a bid day or there was other important business.

Duck hunting was the one sport my dad did with me since I was 10, and I have been hunting them ever since. A long-time business friend Don Ekstrome invited me to join a new duck club called the Manuhui —Hawaiian for bird club. It has been a great bunch of partners and friends for the last 35 years. Duck clubs can be like marriage and not all are good ones, but we are fortunate. As Dad always said, "Class is hard to describe, but you know it when you see it." Don is one of those guys. Knowing I was on the right track and wanting to help me stay on that track, he invited me to join the club.

I first met Don many years before when I was 22. He is a masonry contractor and on one of the office building projects, a misalignment required the wall to be torn down and rebuilt. I could fix it at a much lower cost. I asked Don what the credit would be if he didn't have to redo the block wall. He gave a fair credit and taught me a life lesson at the same time. I asked him what he wanted to do and he said, "Whatever you think is best" putting the decision onto me. We took the credit, a win-win for both. But the lesson taught here is if you want to see their real character, say whatever you think is best in the matter and you will find out. If they are unreasonable you just say no and now you know their true intentions. Great, friend and outstanding person.

Wants and Needs

I took my second wife Linda backpacking on a 68-mile trip with a week layover at Benson Lake. We began the trip at Levitt Meadows about 40 miles north of Benson. On the first day, we had a nice lunch at Poore Lake and Roosevelt Lake with our planned goal of making Fremont Lake that evening. But an hour out on to the trail, she developed altitude sickness and her body was shutting down. I pulled off the trail, found a campsite and stopped for the day. Then gave her water and a little something to eat and she took a nap while I went fishing. The next day's original goal was Dorothy Lake at the summit and the boundary of Yosemite. I had included several layover days in the trek so because we were behind, we made that day's goal, Long Lake.

As we were getting close, it started snowing. She said, "It's snowing, it's snowing." I said, "I know, be thankful it's not raining, keep going." A bit further it started hailing. She turned and said, "It's hailing, it's hailing." "I know. Be thankful it's not raining, keep going." We made it to Long Lake just as the sky let loose with this torrent of rain. She said, "Let's set up the tent." I said, "No, I want to look around to see if there is a better campsite than this one. Give me my poncho and get under this big tree." I quickly ran around the area looking for a better site but found none, so I returned and said we would camp here. She said, "Let's set up the tent." I said, "No, not now." She said, "Why can't we set up the tent?" I said, "Are you getting wet? No! The reason we're not setting up the tent now is because I want it to rain more so we know where the driest spot is and the best place to put the tent."

Well, it made so much sense that it made her mad and she backed up into the base of the tree folding her arms and saying, "What is it about this backpacking that you like?" I said, "You know what, you are not going to know the answer to that question until this trip is over, but I will give you a clue. You are as free as you will ever be because everything you have, need or want is in your pack and on your back. The tent goes there on that dry spot. You can take a nap and I am going fishing." After the week at Benson, she went out with everyone else and Dave Gustafson and I stayed another week and packed through the emigrant wilderness. When she got home, she opened the cupboards and started to cry, realizing that she really didn't need all that stuff. But that faded quickly after she re-acclimated from time in nature to normal city life. The difference between needs and wants!

Following Tracks

During that same trip with Linda, I had to draw upon my tracking knowledge, which comes in handy at times. When we started, I said give me your boots, wherein I took my knife and cut out a notch in the heel of each boot plus cut out one of the diamond nubs in the center of the sole. She said, "What are you doing?" I said, "I am notching your boots so I can tell immediately that it is your track." Well on our trek to Dorothy Lake, she would get out of camp earlier and I would pack up and then catch up. I reviewed the trail and route. I showed her on the map a fork in the trail and told her to take a right at the fork. "If you miss it, there will be a small lake on your right and you will know that you have gone the wrong way at the fork." When I arrived at the fork, her tracks were going left instead of right, so I followed them until they ran out and disappeared with the lake to the right. I backed up and picked up her trail again and followed until it stopped. From there, I started walking in a circle and then spotted her track going up the hill the wrong direction. I followed them to a flat bench where her tracks were quite visible and this man appeared and said, "Are you looking for the woman that made those tracks?" "Yes." "Well, she just started back down 5 minutes ago." I found her sitting, crying on the rock at the fork thinking I had gotten by her. When I walked up, she said, "How did you know I went the wrong way?" I said, "The notches I put in your boot allowed me to follow your tracks."

The Benson Bear

Over the last 30 years, I have been organizing trips into Benson Lake and probably have done 20. There are many stories besides The Bears, but in all the trips that we have made to Benson, we never had any bears until this one particular year, and then we had two. We could hear them on the first night we were there; we could hear the pots and pans clanging and the people yelling down the beach at the first camp, and then the second camp, and then they finally got to our camp. Although we had everything in bear boxes, Juanita's pack still had toothpaste or something in it, so they grabbed her pack and took off into the forest with it. Dave and Steve were running around in the forest in the dark, naked, trying to find stones to throw at the bear and picking up horse poop instead. We finally retrieved the pack, even though the side pocket had been ripped open and the toothpaste removed.

These bears bothered us every night and both of them had tags, so they were bad bears out of the valley that had been relocated. We were sure to put everything away. But one night everything was in the bear boxes, and then there were these cardboard boxes on top of the bear boxes that had the paper towels and napkins and that kind of stuff. Hidden behind the paper towels was a canister of oatmeal. The bear came into camp at night. Nobody heard him. He took those paper towels and he laid them down neatly right in front of the bear boxes. He grabbed that whole container of oatmeal, went to our main fire and sat down.

He didn't crush that box, he unzipped the top, and then glub, glub, glub, glub, glub, ate the whole thing.

I guess probably about the seventh night, it was about 9:30, and Dave Gustafson's son Taylor was sitting directly across the fire from me and I was towards the outside of the camp. All of a sudden, Taylor pointed right over my shoulder and said, "There he is, right there!"

Well, about this time, I had had just about as much of this bear as I wanted, all right. I was pissed off at him. I got up out of my chair, turned 180 degrees and started running at this bear full speed as fast as I could run. At the same time, I was just roaring at him, roaring. He turned and started running, and I was running right next him. I ran him all the way out of camp and there was one point where I was running right by his rear end. I was going to slap him on his rear end, then I said, "Nope, might not be a good idea." At any rate, I chased that bear out of the camp. I came back to the fire and everybody looked at me and said, "Oh, man, you're crazy. You're crazy." But the ironic thing about it is he never came back. Neither of them did. That is the Benson Bear.

One year, I took my friend Charley Meir to Winter Count where I told the bear story around the fire. When I finished, I looked at Charley and said, "I know you have heard that story." He said, "Heard it? What are you talking about? I was there!"

My Children

As I have said a few times, my dad would make a statement or deliver a quip then walk away. One day, Dad walked into my office, stepping right up to the edge of my desk and, in an elevated tone, said, "You think it's tougher being a son than it is being a dad – don't you?" I looked up and said, "There are those occasions." He said, "Well, I have news for you. It's a lot harder being a father than a son. And you're about to find out." Then he turned and walked out.

He was right; it's a lot harder being a parent than it is being a child. I had two children with my first wife, my daughter Candy and my son Tommy, a stepdaughter Lisa in my first marriage and my stepdaughter Amy from my second marriage. I called my beautiful daughter Candy "Sunshine," and I loved waking her up in the morning for the early bus ride to Country Day School. We would have cereal together before she was off on her long day. But these times together were shattered by divorce, making me an every-other-weekend father. My children did not grow up in my house and my stepdaughter Lisa went to live with her dad shortly after I left the house.

Candy was held accountable in her mother's house and has always done well. She graduated from St. Francis High School then got into Cal Poly, but graduated from Saint Marys. I drove her down to help her get everything settled for the start of school. When we were finished and I was about to head home, I gave her a large check to cover all her costs for the semester. One lump sum that had to be budgeted by her. A bit scared and surprised, it freaked her out a bit the responsibility of all that money. Well, it was a good thing she got to go home to her mom's at the end of the semester for Christmas because she was out of money and had maxed out her credit card! I think it was a lesson she never forgot.

While Candy was growing up, I used to tell her all the time, "Candy, don't ask me to get married until you're 30." She made it to 28. The budget for the ceremony was $30,000. I made out the check for my half and gave it to Candy so she had control of it. Upon giving the check to her, I said I want you to think about something for a day and let me know your decision. Do you want to have your big day or do you want a down payment on a house? She chose to have her big day. What a beautiful wedding it was, overlooking Lake Tahoe; it was a gorgeous wedding. About a year later, I asked her in hindsight what she would have done. She said although it was a fantastic wedding, great photos and memories, they could really use it now for their house and in hindsight, it would have been the smarter thing to do. "Wants and needs" and the important choices we make in life.

I am proud of her and her accomplishments, beautiful sunshine to this day. She has been married over 25 years, and has three great children, Max, Will and Talie. She and her husband Bill have done a super job in raising their children; they made them a priority, and it shows. She was not raised in my house and because of that and family dynamics, we are not as close as I would like to be.

Tommy was three years old at the time of the divorce, and I was still drinking during their formative years, not getting sober until he was 10. Tommy had more talent than I ever dreamed of having. He was better than me at everything. He was a great baseball catcher and had a very good bat. When he was 13, I took him to his first major league baseball game at the Oakland A's stadium. We got to our seats and I sat down while Tommy stood there for a minute looking out over the field. Then he turned to me and said, "I can hit it out of here." I said that fence is further than you think. He looked back at me and said again, "I can hit it out of here."

I tried to convey the quips and teaching. But they take time and repetition to be absorbed and that also assumes you're listening. Unlike Candy, but like me, he had no boundaries or accountability in his household, and he did not listen to my sermons on responsibility and right and wrong, risk and consequences. He thought it was all Dad's bullshit and did not recognize or have the invisible wall to stop from pushing the limits too far. I nicknamed him "10 plan" because he was always unrealistically planning to do too many things in one day. Today, we will go skiing in Tahoe and then to a concert in San Jose with eight other things to do in between.

He was a good catcher and, at 13, was given an opportunity to be starting catcher and play in the higher division with the older kids, a real opportunity. But instead, he pushed the limits, went to Tahoe, and decided to climb Eagle Rock in his shorts and Teva sandals. Well, when you push the limits too much, the odds of something going wrong go way up and it did. He fell 35 feet to the rocks below and injured himself badly. But it is amazing the healing power of youth and he recovered. However, it put an end to his baseball.

Some six months after the accident, we were driving home from a duck hunting trip, and I tried to use the time as a teachable moment. I said, "I can't wait to hear your fall-off-the-cliff story when you're 40!" He said, "What are you talking about? It will be the same as it is today." I said, "Oh, no it won't. You will have a better perspective on the damage your behavior has caused you and your body. Your perspective right now is that you're not going to be 40 and you're certainly never going to die and you are wrong on both counts." Surprisingly, at 40, he still had no clue, despite the pain in his body caused by all the hairline fractures and damage throughout that resulted from the fall.

I had a good relationship with my wife Linda's daughter, Amy, who lived in our house. Amy is a very talented, smart, and focused young woman that I had a great relationship with until my divorce from her mother, which sadly made it impossible to continue.

My dad had watched over the years and he could see what was coming from a mile away. You know, you can lead a horse to water, but you can't make them drink. I know. For many years, I tried on many occasions and from many different directions and angles. But sometimes you can't even get them to the water. At that point, you just have to let them go find their own path.

Despite your own mistakes, we do the best we can to teach our children and protect, support and guide them into their future world. But ultimately, each child has to find their own path with the choices they make. Sometimes, that is hard to watch.

So, he was absolutely correct that it is harder being a parent than it is being a child.

Your Tracks

During the time I was back with Linda, my interest in primitive skills increased, I took several tracking classes that improved my awareness of the tracking knowledge I already had.

Amy, my stepdaughter was a very self-motivated young lady, but I always let her mom do the disciplining. It was kind of my standard to just supervise. I didn't really get too much involved, that was up to her mom. But every once in a while, I'd stop Amy in passing and say, "You know what, Sweetie? You may be blowing this by your mom, but you're not blowing it by me."

I'd do that every once in a while, and she'd kind of give me a dirty look. Once when her mom and I returned from a week's vacation, I went to make a pot of coffee and Amy was in the utility room, ironing some clothes. She said, "You guys left the coffee grounds in there all week, and they got all moldy."

I said, "Oh, did you discover that on your final cleanup?"

"Excuse me?"

I said, "You know, the final cleanup before the parents come home?"

"You don't know what you're talking about."

I said, "Amy, I have been telling you for years that you can blow it by your mom, but you're not blowing it by me. And this time, I will prove it to you. One, you're really good at cleaning up all your tracks, but you still leave light wipe marks."

She just blew it off. So, a couple days later, she was talking to her mom about a problem because she backed my car into a friend's Volkswagen. She thought she was going to be able to fix it, but the guy was being unreasonable, so I heard about it. I said, "Well, when you guys get done talking, maybe you and I will go have a little conversation." They finished and I took her into her bedroom and I said, "Sweetheart, you know what? I am not going to ask you what happened last week. I am going to tell you, and this is how it goes. You had your friends over the night we left. And there were only three or four of them, and that went just fine. That was Thursday night. You decided to have the party on Friday. So, you had one Friday, and you had one Saturday. The Saturday one started getting out of control."

I could see the tears starting to come down her cheeks. I said, "You got honey in the peanut butter, for example."

She said, "Well, I didn't put it in the peanut butter."

"I know you didn't put the honey in the peanut butter. What you don't know is, you don't know who did. So, let us look at this, okay? Not only did you have the party, but you left kids in the house while you were gone, and in your excitement to make whatever connection you were going to make, you backed into the guy's car."

The next day, I found a bottle cap under the fireplace poker, so as my mother used to do, I just stuck it on her pillow. Then, a couple days later, I found a wine cooler in the back of my car, and I was no longer drinking. I took the wine cooler, and I took one of those Post-It notes. I drew a paw print on it with a note that said, "found another track, this one is in the mud", and I stuck it on her pillow.

She brought home a friend and the friend looked at this wine cooler with this note on it on her pillow. She said, "Amy, what does this mean?"

Amy said, "Oh, it's a long story. I will tell you later."

After about two weeks, I got a really nice card from Amy saying, "You know, you're right. I didn't believe you, but you definitely made me a believer." Some time later, I think it was Christmas or her birthday, I took a piece of soapstone, and I carved a paw print in it and made it into a pendant, wrapped it up in a little square box, and put a note with it that said, "Just remember, your tracks will follow you for the rest of your life."

My Brother's Death

The impact of my brother Bill's death and view of his life made it clearer to me that I needed to start following my heart's desire to get off this conveyer belt of having to be the best, trying to keep up with the persona of having to make the most money, live in the biggest house and drive the fanciest cars. What did it do for him? But even then, it took years to complete the change. I no longer wanted to strive to be the biggest and the best. It was no longer important to me and I didn't need to prove anything.

Regrettably, my brother and I were never close, even as kids, and sadly it was a love-hate relationship. Because he was my big brother, I looked up to him and tried to emulate him. In the beginning of work, he taught me much about banking and financing, strategizing and planning, but because of the inequality of our ownership eventually resulted in being estranged for 15 years. He had places and traveled all over the world: a home in Aspen; a ranch in Montana; an apartment in New York; and trips to Europe, Greece and Mexico. Through the years, he would check on me from afar or through someone. Many times, he sent someone I knew to stop by out of the blue, just to say hi and to check on how I was doing. As if I didn't recognize what he was doing. I, on the other hand, just watched and listened to people to get a picture of how he was doing. He was a very wealthy man who at one point, took on more than he could carry prior to an economic downturn, but rumor was, years before that, he had gotten into cocaine, flittering all over the place and not paying attention to his business.

There were years of losses and my brother let the older WITH Corporation office buildings go into foreclosure. I could not allow that to happen, as the taxes on the forgiveness of the debt would have wiped me out. So, in a last-ditch effort, I traded my 10% in all of the buildings for 100% of one office building and pulled it out of foreclosure. As more years passed, it became obvious to me that he was in big trouble and I needed to try to help him. Remember, this was an emotional love-hate relationship that had been estranged for the last 15 years.

So, I bought a card that said on the outside **"No matter where you go..."** Then on the inside, it said, **"there you are."** I wrote, "Bill, you can go to Aspen, you can go to Mexico, you can go to New York or Greece, but you're not going to get away from YOU! I know you're in trouble and if you would like your bother's help, call me." A short time later, he called and I, along with help from Dad, convinced him to come home and get sober and he did. But shortly after, he rented a nice place in Santa Barbara and isolated himself again. So many times over the years, I just wanted to drop him in the middle of nowhere with me to show him what life is really about and the difference between wants and needs. And let nature teach him about living. You know, we work for a living, but the Indians lived for a living with Family, community and ceremony!

He had been diagnosed with bipolar condition, which may help explain much of his behavior. I spent the next three months talking with him on the phone and made one trip down to Santa Barbara for four days. While there, I became somewhat depressed because of his lack of life. I said, "Bill you have a wonderful place here, a great view, but you have no life and no wonder you are depressed." But I could not get him to come home. The man had all the wealth one could ever need, or want, he had a lot of money, but he had nothing; he had no life, no lifelong friends, no partner or wife, no real home base and he ended up taking his own life at 50.

I am beginning to realize that his bipolar condition could have begun way back when we were kids. With this realization, I am finding it a little easier to understand and forgive. He was very successful moneywise, but is that success? Success to me is having all that you need and being happy with it; the wants are just good fortune and icing on the cake.

After my brother's death and over some time, I really realized the load was too much. I wasn't enjoying the high style and the strain it took to hold that up. I had too much in my pack. So, I needed to have more balance and support than I was getting. I moved out again, resulting in the divorce of my second wife. I left her in the fabulous 40s with the Mercedes and moved to a one-bedroom apartment for the next four years and began unpacking my pack, so to speak. It was no longer important to me to make more and more money for more and more stuff. My interest and understanding had slowly changed.

Clear the Office

Before his death, my brother had dictated and recorded a new will that he had transcribed and had his housekeeper sign and witness his signature. The new will gave me the Sacramento Outing Duck Club and made me a co-executor of his estate. Dad assumed that as executor, I could resolve his longstanding money disputes that he had with my brother.

But a will must have two witnesses to be valid and because of that, it was invalid and reverted back to a previous will. My dad walked into my office and, in a demanding tone, said I was responsible for correcting the monetary issues he thought were my brother's fault. Although it was an unrealistic and impossible demand, I said, "Well, sit down and we will discuss it." But he didn't sit down and his tone got louder as he repeated his demand. I said we were not going to have a conversation until you sit down, my own anger surfacing. Again, he wouldn't sit down, got angrier, and his face turned red. With my anger in full force, I stood up and, in a stern voice, said, "You either sit down or I am going to come around this desk and sit you down." With that, we cleared everyone from the office.

I proceeded to quickly come around my desk and go right at my dad. Now remember, he was 6 feet and I am 5' 8" so as I got close, I stepped slightly to the left and swung my right leg in behind the back of his leg at the knee joint. In a judo move, I just pushed on his shoulders and followed him falling backwards into the chair. Then I started yelling at him in a very loud and angry voice saying, "How does it make you feel to have someone yelling in your face? Does my angry face look becoming to you? You do this all the time and this is what it looks like!" Then I walked out of the office and left him in the chair. Some time later, we had our discussion where I explained the impossibility and unfairness of his demands that were out of my control.

Followed His Path

My brother and I were successful by seizing the opportunities afforded us by our fathers just like Dad's success was afforded him by his father. He was removed from spending time with his children because of work, success, and his increased drinking. Same thing with me: too busy trying to be successful to spend more time with my kids and being a drunk during their formative years. As I said, being a divorced-every-other-weekend father combined with family dynamics has not made for the closest relationships. But I have always been there

I did not realize, or was just in denial of the damage my dad's alcoholism did to the family, until I looked back at it while writing this book. I never got mad at my dad for the damage it did, maybe because I did not want to recognize it even though the feelings were there. One day while driving home after one of our lunches, the radio played Harry Chapin's "Cat's in the Cradle," and I told him to listen to the words because I wanted him to see he was not there for me and to show him the kind of childhood I had with him. He didn't like it because it was true. As the song says, "As he hung up the phone, it occurred to me that my boy was 'just like me.'" It is amazing how many times you follow the lineage of your dad.

My friend Steve Crowle hated his dad for making him do the lawn and garden at his house. He hated doing it and fought with his dad about it. But what did he do for a living? Landscaping and maintenance. What your family does may have an influence on what you end up doing. Family races cars, there is a good chance you will probably be in that sport. The same applied to me and I followed his track most of my life including the alcoholic stage. But I was fortunate enough to have my other hobbies and interests and his help to stop 15 years earlier in life than he did, allowing me that much more time to grow and enjoy life.

While striving to be successful and live up to the teachings in 1975, "work, work, work" like Dad, I built what might be called my Parkridge house. It was a 3,700 sq.-ft. home I built on an acre of land in Fair Oaks on Buchanan Drive. I moved 3,500 cubic yards of dirt to build the house pad, party pad and pool pad as it sloped down toward the small creek in the center. On the other side of the creek, I cut in a pad for a future tennis court. The house was 105 feet across the front with two offset ridge rooflines and a flat roof in between with a pop-up clear story over the living and dining room. From the back, it looked like the 19th hole of a fancy clubhouse with full glass windows overlooking the land, just like the Parkridge house. We didn't stay long because my alcohol and drug use caused major problems, so I sold it in 1975 for $275,000. That is a lot of money for the time but shows what a terrific home it was.

After we sold the Buchanan house, we moved to Park Road. Just off of Auburn Blvd. in kind of a secluded horse property area with acre+ parcels in the middle of the city. After closing the deal, we had to remodel it before moving in. During the 2 months of remodel, we lived in our 22' motorhome on the land behind the house, all 5 of us, and it again was a happy time. Sometime after moving into the house, we went out for Sunday breakfast.

Upon returning, I pulled into the garage on the side of the house with its door into the hallway that lead to the kitchen-family room area. Upon entering, I noticed the front door was wide open, then I noticed the stool at the kitchen counter had been moved and there were tracks in the freshly mopped red tile floor that my Haley had done before going breakfast. Then I discovered the sliding glass door to my son's room had been jimmied open, but nothing was missing. I called the police to report the break-in and that nothing was missing. A short time later, I was watching TV in the den and for some reason, I picked up the photo album. As I went through the pages, I noticed pictures of my wife missing.

I asked her, "Did you give one of your sisters any pictures?" She said, "No." I immediately picked up the phone, called the police and told them about the missing pictures. They were out at house within a minute.

This was 1976, and they had been after a man that had been terrorizing the community, raping and murdering people. He would break into occupied family homes, tie the husband up with plates on his back and if they fell, he would shoot his wife, then he would take her to the living room and sodomize her. In our area, he was known as the "east area rapist" or the "golden state killer."

We spent months staying up to wee hours of the morning expecting an attack. Hell, I slept with a pistol under my pillow. He never came back, but I think that is because we caught him casing the house, which was part of his MO and he did not want to take the risk. Thank God we surprised him because had we not, he may have returned! He eluded law enforcement for 35 years until just recently in 2020 when they matched his DNA to multiple (50) rapes and (13) murders and has been arrested. Joseph De Angelo pled guilty to avoid the trial and death penalty for his absolute reign of terror on the state of California and Sacramento in particular and will be sentenced to life in prison without parole. It was a really scary time. Shortly after that, we divorced and sold that house.

While building the Buchanan house, we rented a small house close by to monitor the construction. Years after, it occurred to me I was happier in the little rental house and the motor home than I was in the big fancy house. Even though that had occurred to me, I kept going after the high life even years later with the weekend kids, and my second wife Linda wanted a bigger house. So, we moved to a much bigger more expensive house. putting more weight in my pack to carry. It was a big house but not homey. The marriage was not working very well and I was lonely in my own home and stressed in business and cash flow needed to carry the load. Shortly thereafter, we sold it, separated and I moved out to a 1-bedroom apartment. But then, as I said before, when I broke my back I moved back in with Linda in a house in McKinley. Shortly after that, we were back in the fab 40s on 43rd street and living the high style life again.

Even though it had occurred to me that I didn't like big houses, I still kept buying them. I divorced Linda and years later, my wife Sandy and I bought a small 2-bedroom love cottage south of Folsom Blvd.; we are much happier. Then we moved to another small 2-bedroom on 55th because of the backyard and room for our large vegetable garden.

Although I followed Dad's path in many ways, I diverged from it in many other ways because I am my own individual and have my own desires, interests, imagination and wants. The many interests that Mom promoted and encouraged (see Mom and Self Reliance) set me on a different path, but the one that really got me turned around was my primitive skills interest, the teachings and view of life absorbed from all my friends at Rabbitstick and Winter Count. Then implementation came with Sandy's help and balance. It took years and is still on going—welcome to the Tom and Sandy show! As I said, Dad didn't have any hobbies, and in the end, I got him to plant a tomato plant in a pot on his patio. I wish I had gotten him to do that years before because the process of it growing and then producing brought him amazement and joy.

Get Mad and You Lose

I got my temper and facial expressions from my dad. First, the jaw starts pulsing, then the face turns red and the eyes dilate. It took me a long time to learn to control my temper, and, as dad always said, "If you get into a fight and you get mad, you will lose the fight." That's not necessarily a fist fight; it could be an argument or a dispute. You get mad and you lose. Been there, done that. It can be a costly mistake. Dad did not always practice what he preached on this one!

On the other hand, sometimes it can work in your favor. Dave Perrault loves to tell this story of his out-of-control client and what not to do in a deposition. Dave was representing my brother's estate in a claim. My brother had met a new person at an AA meeting who had become his glorified babysitter and traveling companion. My brother bought him new fancy clothes, a Harley Davidson motorcycle and trips here and there. Then gave him a job during the four months he was in Santa Barbara until his death. This guy sued because he thought he was entitled to something. Well, I was really pissed off at this guy, and I told Dave I would take a calm deposition, but warned him that if the man's lawyer opened the door, I was going to lambast her.

Toward the end of the deposition, she opened the door for me and I took her head off for representing this loser. I started by calmly saying that she, his attorney, appeared to me to be a very sharp and intelligent lawyer. Then I tore into her for representing this money grabber with no claim and how could such a sharp attorney be dumb enough to think there is anything here? He is nothing but a glorified gigolo and caretaker of my brother who was sick and is now dead. My brother had employees who had worked for him for 25 years and none of them were suing, but this guy with three months is entitled to nothing. Finally, you can be sure that I will instruct the estate to vigorously defend and you will waste your time, lose the case and your client has no money to pay you, so wise up. The deposition ended shortly thereafter and the case settled that afternoon.

In another case, the carpenter's union was suing on their claim against my subcontractor. First impressions mean a lot and I did not want to appear as a big contractor so I wore my work jeans and t-shirt and my work boots to the deposition as if I had just gotten out of my truck. The owner's attorney said to me, "You're not at all what I expected." Well, the room was full of attorneys representing their clients, the owners, subcontractor, the union and myself and my attorney. The deposition took all day and then they finally got to me. After a few questions had been asked and answered, the union attorney asked me if I provided the owners with a lien free project. I answered, "Yes." Somewhat confused, he said, "We have a lien against the project. How did you provide them with a lien free job?" I said, "Simple. I bonded around your lien." With that, the light went on in every attorney's head that it was clear the Union was suing the wrong party and now there was not enough time to refile the case against the bonding company. So they dropped it.

Life Lessons Learned: Make the Deal and Move On

In my experience and looking back it occurred to me that when you are in dispute over some issue and no matter what side of the table you are on, the best thing you can do is unload the wagon, take the loss and move on. If the lawyers get involved, even if you win your point, you lose due to the cost of the attorneys. Say there is a dispute of $300,000, before the attorneys get involved, call the opposing party and set up a meeting to try and resolve the issue.

Put your tail between your legs, forget the principle of the point and leave your ego at the door to make a deal, take the loss and move on, and you will be far ahead. In a typical dispute, the attorney fee to get the issue just to mediation would cost each party $80,000-$100,000, then you end up settling somewhere towards the middle and both parties lose. It is worth a try to resolve now for about the same dollars but not near the continued time to litigate the dispute. Had I recognized this earlier, it would have saved me a lot of stress, time and money.

We had built a condominium project in Pinole and had already spent thousands of dollars trying to find and fix leaks that occurred at the fireplace and nearby plugs. The attempts to repair things were unsuccessful and we were about to get into a huge lawsuit with the owner, which would bring in the expert from afar and probably would have resulted in tearing off the stucco, and replacing windows. It was going to be ugly and expensive. I know you cannot fix a leak unless you know exactly where it is leaking from. I called the owner, set up a meeting and asked him to hold off on filing the suit and give me the opportunity to see if I can find the problem. He agreed.

I took a crew and we poured water on the building starting at the bottom and working our way to the top. All the walls and around the windows, the fireplace chimneys and flashing. We worked all day and could not get a drop of water in to the building. Then we got to the roof. Flood the roof, still no leakage? Then I was applying water to the parapet wall above the second floor. It was late in the day and the Bay Area Pinole winds started to pick up. I noticed the water dropping from vane to vane in the wall vent was being blown into the building, so I sprayed the vent directly. Immediately, we had water at the fireplace and nearby plug. We spent $3,000 installing vent covers on the specified vents and saved a multimillion-dollar suit.

You're Picking on the Wrong Motherfucker Tonight

Sandy and I had gone to a party for one of the employees that was moving back to New York. She had some papers we had to go over to be signed before she went home, so we left the party. It was about 9:00. We stopped at Bradshaw's on Sunrise, to have a cup of coffee and take care of the paperwork.

Upon leaving, we approached the parking lot drive, and there was a car coming down the drive. It stopped and they waved us to go ahead. Sandy's car was on the right, mine was on the left, and we were in between them; she was behind me. I think we were going to have a cigarette and talk for a little bit and then she was going to go home. Anyway, I was opening the passenger door when I heard this voice say, "Give me your money."

The door was open, so I took one step sideways to my left, I reached behind me, pulled on Sandy and pushed her towards the open door. Putting me in the middle and she was on the far side. I put her in the passenger seat and shut the door. Then I turned to this guy and stepped right up into striking distance and said, "Excuse me? You need directions where?"

This guy was holding a pearl-handled silver six-shooter. It looked like the Lone Ranger's cap gun. For a nanosecond, I wanted to throw my right hand at him and knock him out. But the voice on my shoulder said, "You better be 100% sure that you can knock him out because he has the gun." I stepped back a couple of steps. He wanted his money and it was taking too much time. The driver was then getting out of the car and yelling at me over the trunk of his car "Give him your money now, Fucker."

I don't know what happens when somebody does this to me, but you don't do this to me. I wanted to take that gun away from that guy and unload six bullets into him for doing that to me. At any rate, the driver was saying, "Just give him your money."

At about a volume 10, I said, "NO! You guys are picking the wrong motherfucker tonight." I started walking toward the guy with the gun. He retreated around the corner of my car backing up into his open passenger door. I came out from behind my car and I saw him backing into the seat, pointing the gun right at me. So, I ducked back behind the corner of my Blazer. Boom! You could see that one-foot flame coming out of that barrel; it was no cap gun! And then off they went. The police finally showed up and said, "Next time, just give them the money."

Balance Needed

I found the balance I needed in my third wife Sandy, and she has helped me tremendously. She grabbed hold of this wild horse, put a corral around me and calmed me down quite a bit. She's very cautious, whereas I am a risk taker. That causes us conflict from time to time, but we work it out. She came from a life completely different from the one I was raised in. She had more boundaries at 18 than I did when I was five. Her father was a teamster worker and didn't make the big money. But they always had what they needed.

Like the tortoise and the hare, in the end her mother actually had more in assets than my mom and dad had together. Making it clear that life is not a sprint, it's a marathon, plan and budget for the long haul. They bought everything with cash and never owned credit with the exception of the house. Very Smart approach. All you need is a little patience. Sandy's mom raised her two older brothers when their parents died early then raised her own family. If they wanted something, they had an envelope or a can to save money for it and when they had enough, they paid cash for it. Whereas I was taught to leverage money, but leveraging money doesn't always work for you. Sometimes you find yourself being the leaf at the end of the branch when the wind's blowing. I didn't want to continue being that blown leaf at the end of the branch, and I needed support and balance. Sandy provided much of that for me along with all her teachings and her perceptions. The way she was raised certainly gave me a different perspective on life, on what's important. I had been trying to keep up with the Joneses and not enjoying a minute of it. So, with Sandy's help, I think I've changed for the better. She made me a better man.

I'm still a risk-taker and wild child. With my ADD and hyperactivity, I can go spinning and just take off. As Sandy said the other day," if it wasn't for me you may be dead," And you know what? She might be right. Who knows? Getting together with Sandy really helped me get a little balanced, as she kind of broke me down and pulled on my reins. Had that not happened, maybe I would have started drinking again. All I know is her influence and her balance is a very positive influence on me. Because I am always pushing the limits. "You can't do that." "Yes, I can, I am Tom Cook."

The General

Sandy's very much like her mother Juanita, who in her 90s was 4'11" and was called the General. We would drive down to San Mateo so Sandy could help her go shopping on the weekends. She never drove. When they went shopping, it was 9:00, not 8:58; it was 9:00, every time. One time, she gave me some chores to do in the backyard.

When they returned from shopping, the garage door was open and she could see through it to where I was working. She got out of the car with her cane, scurried through the door right up to me and said, "What are you doing?" I said, "Well, I'm doing what you told me to do." She said, "No, no, you're out here without a hat, you don't have gloves on, and you're sweating like a pig." Then she turned around to Sandy and said, "Get this man a towel." In a few minutes, I had hat, gloves, and towel. Another time, I was disposing of some clippings. I guess I put some clippings into the trash instead of the clipping can. She said, "Those don't go in there. They go in the other can."

I said, "Juanita, it's just a stick. Nobody's going to know." She said, "Yes they will, we have inspectors here." I said, "Really." She said, "Yes they do, and the inspector is standing right in front of you and that can's not going into the street until it goes in the right can."

Sandy is very much like her mom; that's when I call her Juanita.

Every Form of Refuge Has Its Price

One of the most important things I learned with the help of Sandy and my primitive skills family is the difference between needs and wants. Do you really need it? I had been buying things we didn't need with money I didn't have to impress people we didn't know. It just didn't make sense, but that's where I was before.

My wife Sandy was at Rabbitstick with me once, and we were talking with my friend Kayla Michaels who said, "I think I will go down to Arizona this winter for a couple months." Sandy said, "Well what about your bills?" Kayla said, "WHAT BILLS? I don't have any bills. I don't have car, insurance or a phone. My rent is already paid so I have no bills! I am free to go and come as I please and I just got back from a 2-month trip to Alaska." "Every form of refuge has its price" (Eagles). One of my favorite sayings. Whether rich or poor, there is a price to be paid. Over the years, my wife has brought me a more balanced life. Sometime I buck because she is more cautious than I want to be, but there is nothing wrong with being conservative.

We're completely different and came from completely different worlds. We've been together 24 years and married almost 20. Therefore, there's a certain amount of compromise that takes place. I may not agree with what she's saying, but I've learned that rather than say, "Oh that's not right" or "No, you're wrong." I'll say, "You might be right" but we can look at it from this angle or from this view. Makes a conversation go a lot easier.

I keep threatening to put two cameras in our kitchen, which would be the stage for the new TV hit, The Tom and Sandy show. From time to time, when we are discussing an issue with different points of view, I look up at the corner where the cameras should be and say "Welcome to The Tom & Sandy Show."

I wish I had already done it years ago, as they would be classics. An example of this, although not in the kitchen, was when I took Sandy backpacking for the first time. On the trail, we came to a small creek crossing with slow moving water about 12 inches deep. There was a 10-inch log crossing. I walked across, turned around, motioned and said, "Come across the log." She would not do it. I crossed back over to her side, stuck out my hand and said, "I will guide you across. She wouldn't. I don't remember what it was, but I think she was afraid of falling off the log into the stream. So, I crossed back to the other side, took my pack off and then went back to her again. When I got to her, I unsnapped her waist belt and then her chest clip, reached over her head and pulled her pack off her back then walked it to the other side. I returned with a guiding hand out and she still would not cross.

My patience ran out and I said, "Camp is another two miles up the trail and I don't care how you get across this stream but I will meet you in camp. You figure it out." With that, I picked up my pack and headed out leaving her standing on the other side. I walked a couple hundred yards up the trail to a large rock that I climbed up on and could now see the trail all the way back to the crossing.

In a couple minutes I could see her coming up the path just madder than a pistol and stomping the ground like an angry bull with each step she took. So, here she comes stomping up the trail. Then she raises her head enough to see me standing on this boulder watching her. This made her stomp even harder. When she got to me, I said, "Sweetheart, you need to trust in what I am telling you to do" "NO!" she said, "You need to be sensitive to my fears and concerns—you have been backpacking since you were a kid and you expect me to have the same confidence as you? On my first trip?" "Ok, point made and I am sorry, but you still need to trust in what I tell you."

Another time, we had a tenant who was in trouble with the law and the district attorney wanted me as a possible witness so they needed to serve me. I said sure and gave them our address for service. Sandy got all concerned that the tenant would get our address. I said, "Not to worry, they can't get our address." "Yes, they can and it scares me." "No, they can't. This is coming from the district attorney's office." She said, "I am still concerned." I said, "Don't be." And she replied, "Don't be bald." Stopped me in my tracks. Point made. That's how she feels.

After-Work Chats

Over the 25 years that dad was in my office, many times after the workday was over, Dad would come to my office and we would discuss current matters, issues or problems at hand. On one occasion, we were talking or strategizing on a deal he was working on. While I was talking, all of a sudden, this smirk appeared and morphed into a smile on his face. I said, "What are you smiling about?" He said, shaking his head a bit, "Deja vu! You remind me of my father (my grandfather)!"

"What do you mean?" "Oh, just the way you approached the problem, your mannerisms, the way you move and talk. Just made me think of your grandfather." Happened three or four times. These after-work conversations or lunches at the Sutter Club occurred 2-3 times a month and covered the gamut of subjects, deals, strategies and sermon repeats. He was old school and I could never get him to come up in the times. But he had lost 20 years, which makes it difficult.

He was a handshake deal maker from the old days and good at it. "I know dad, but that's not the way it's done today!" "Dad, if the numbers don't work, it won't fly and you can't just trust your gut anymore." He was a sales man. He sold the Chinese government to bring him to China for three months as a consultant at their cost. I regret not going with him.

Dad had class and lived his life the way he wanted. His favorite song was Frank Sinatra's "I Did It My Way." And he did. In the later years, I knew he was running low on money, so I tried to convey my change in philosophy to him, the difference between needs and wants. I had tried on many occasions to get him to come off the high style of living, sell the big house in the Fab 40s and live in a more moderate sustainable way. He didn't have the funds to sustain it for very long, but as hard as I tried over the years, he would not change. In the end, he was running out of money. I was very worried about his inability to survive and the extra burden that would be required to make sure he had enough to live on. I believe this reality caused extreme stress on his life and marriage resulting in his cancer.

BE CAREFUL WHAT YOU WISH FOR

This is not an original but it is so very true and Dad said it all the time. As an example

When the new TV program called Naked and Afraid first came out, I wanted to sign up. I was working on my application for the program on my computer and was about ten seconds from hitting the send button when Sandy walked up and said, "What are you doing?" I told her I was filling out my application for Naked and Afraid.

"I don't think so!" She said.

"Why not? It's been my passion for 30 years."

She said, "You are not going with another woman for 21 days, let alone naked. Who's going to take care of you when you come home with a deadly bug bite or parasite?"

As much as I sometimes hate it, she gives me balance and she was right because they put you in places without many resources, and they are more interested in the drama than in the skills.

Be very careful what you wish for.

You might get it.

Then what?

QUIP: TIP OF MY FINGER

One of his last quips towards the end of his life was "You can put everything I know on the tip of my finger." I think it was about not considering yourself to be all that important in the whole scope of things; you're just a humble little part. At least that's how I interpret it, as there was no sermon behind it. I think it meant BE HUMBLE. No matter who you are or what you have done in the whole scope of things, you can put it all on the tip of your finger.

Life changes very slowly, if it ever changes at all, kind of like rocks doing a slow dance. It took a long while to change my perceptions of life from what I had been taught. I am not saying his teachings weren't good, but there was too much emphasis on money and winning and not enough about life and love, nurturing and balance. What do you want: more money or more time? It took a long time to recognize and make the transition and change.

NEVER GOING TO GET ANGRY AGAIN

My dad's hip had been hurting him and he was limping; for some time, he had been going to the doctor, trying to figure out what was wrong. I thought maybe he needed to go to the chiropractor because his back had gotten out of whack and it was pinching a nerve or something, affecting his hip. They did all this testing, I mean, tons and tons of testing. They took a biopsy of his lung and nothing showed up. Then one night, when he was getting up from saying his prayers at his Ottoman, he broke his good leg. I had just been over at his house. I had told him, "Dad, I'm going to go to Tahoe. Everything is going to be all right. Are you going to be fine?"

When he broke his leg, the door was locked, and he couldn't get to the phone. He finally got a hold of Charlie Meir who took him to the hospital. They discovered bone marrow with a very aggressive cancer.

When I was visiting him at Gramercy Court one time, we were sitting in the courtyard outside facing each other, having a conversation when he leaned forward from his wheelchair and started pointing his finger at me as he did many times when he wanted my attention, "Tommy, Tommy, from this day forward, I'm never going to get angry again."

"Really, Dad?"

"No, no, no. I mean it."

"Well, that is really good, Dad, I am happy for you."

A few days later, I was taking him to the doctor. I said, "Hey, Dad, the other day you said you were never going to get angry again." In not even a nanosecond, he popped up and said, "Absolutely. I used to think it worked for me. It doesn't work at all. It's not a good thing. I might get excited, but I am never going to get angry again." I said, "Tell me something. Where are you getting this new information from?"

He said, "Well, I'm 77 years old. I am dying of cancer, and "I guess, I can just hear better!" (Mom's angel).

Life Regrets

After Dad was diagnosed with cancer, he was at Gramercy Court, an elderly care facility with a two-month diagnosis to live, I went to see him one afternoon. He was facing away from the door with his back towards me. He did not hear me approach and I could tell he was in deep thought, so I stopped and stood in the doorway and watched him for a few minutes. He was sitting in his wheelchair with his head bowed down, then all of a sudden, his head would spring back as he let out a big ah!! Sigh. He did this several times over the next few minutes until he realized I was there. I think I know what he was doing; I think he was agonizing over some of his life mistakes and regrets.

Sure, there are lots of regrets that woulda, coulda, shoulda, but didn't–missed opportunities, wrong decisions – wrong perceptions – it's water under the bridge.

Like Paul Simon's song, "A bad day is when I think about the way things might have been." Regretting is a waste of time unless you learn something from it or can do something about it.

We have all had them and they can hurt internally when we recognize our own mistakes, but it is good that you do. "Knock yourself down" so you can pick yourself up and be a better person. That day, we talked about life and death, the inequities of the world, religion, God and dying, heaven and hell. And we reminisced of good times and triumphs.

A Significant Dream

Close to the end after his diagnosis and after one of our conversations, I had told him of a dream I had where everyone went to bed and woke up purple. But that it did not fix the racial problem because in a short period of time, mankind developed the classification and prejudices in the big ears, skinny lips, pointed noses etc. That night I had what I call a significant dream.

The Dream

Mohammed, Jesus, Moses, Buddha, all of the prophets of the world in the past, all show up around the world simultaneously: Vatican Square, Tiananmen Square, Washington DC, Los Angeles, San Francisco, Tokyo. They're on every single screen, every radio station. Mohammed stepped forward as if he was going to a microphone that was not there, and he started to speak. No matter what language you spoke, he was speaking your language. He stepped up and said, "We are here because you people do not understand that we are all teaching the same thing. And because you haven't got it, let me make it simple for you. Love your god, love your neighbor and love yourself. Stop fighting over religion, as you all are worshipping the same god. We will be back to check on your progress." And they disappeared.

Six months went by and we had done absolutely nothing. So, they reappeared and said, "You have done absolutely nothing. Therefore, we are going to start taking the steps and punishing you for your sins, no matter what they are. It will be obvious to the world when you are punished as to what you're being punished for. We are going to begin with the murderers. If you have murdered somebody, tomorrow you will be a pile of dirt."

Then the dream flashed to death row prison cells. In the first cell, there was a pile of dirt. In the second cell, there was a pile of dirt. In the third cell, a guy was standing there. And the dream ended. It was a significant dream.

It is beyond me why we need to fight each other over religious beliefs yet we have been doing it for thousands of years. The prophets of the past have all been preaching that. It seems we are not listening.

Pray for a Parking Space

This was not so much a quip as it was a suggestion, a suggestion to make contact with your God. This was backed up in our years of conversations.

You're late for the appointment and can't find a parking spot. Pray for a parking space and all of a sudden, one will show up. Make contact, ask for guidance and I will receive it from the voice on my shoulder.

I was raised in the Catholic religion and believe in Jesus Christ, God the father, and the Holy Spirit, but I became disillusioned by the age of 18. I was pissed off at the Catholic religion for all the man-made guilt bullshit they tried to lay upon our shoulders. I believe in churches, not church. I am not going to hell if I don't go to church.

I can go to church or talk to my God anytime, anywhere. I just don't do it enough. I could write pages on this from the baloney sandwich on Friday to the mortal sins. Example, we were taught that you could not go to another faith's church. Hmmm. If a good man of a different faith is exposed to the Catholic religion and does not convert then he will not go to heaven! Really? I did not give up on my own beliefs. My Jesus would never turn away a good person of another faith, but would say move forward through the gate, my good man.

You will notice that I said move forward through the gate because what I believe in simplistic terms is, I do not think we go from here straight to heaven at light speed while still burdened by the 7 deadly sins! I think it's a long journey and we are at the lower end of the totem pole with much to learn and far to go. (As my dad said, "more will be revealed.") And it will. Have faith. I think if you're a good person, you move forward in the journey to heaven. The bad people don't move forward, but rather move backwards and the results of that new life somewhere could be hell as it is for some people here! Jesus is the son of God, but aren't we all sons and daughters of God, the first mover and creator? I believe the Holy Spirit is all around because it is the connective spirit that lives in the soul of everyone. Like Brother Justin said, "There had to be a first mover and lastly, you must have faith."

THING TO PONDER

I loved playing in the dirt with my Tonka toys. I liked playing with water in the dirt and moving and grading dirt to make one channel flow over another then rejoining it downstream. Although at the time I didn't know it, it gave me an understanding of civil engineering (i.e., cut and fill) and an understanding of elevations. While playing in the dirt I had gotten a magnet and ran it through the dirt and it picked up iron filings!

As a kid, I was always inquisitive about how things were made or how they worked. Because of that, Mom bought me several HOW TO books, books that had information on how and why things worked as they did. Ever since collecting iron filings by dragging a magnet through the dirt at home and the schoolhouse dirt in the first grade, I have been intrigued with magnets and the force that keeps them apart. That curiosity morphed into what I call **"a thing to ponder,"** because even today, we don't know what the repelling force really is.

When as a child, we took two magnets and put north to north and south to south and they would not go together. They repel each other and we don't know what that force is. We know that when we spin it, we can create electricity. And we can manipulate it, but we do not know precisely what the force is. The "thing to ponder" is whatever that force is, whatever it really is, it's the answer! It's the answer to all kinds of things yet to be discovered.

When I started thinking about this as a youngster, we did not have magnetic imaging and magnetic tape and magnetic strips or Maglev bullet trains. Every year as I have grown, I read or heard about a new use of magnetism, I thought, it's the use of that force, or a thing to ponder, maybe even to reason how the universe works as it does. So, as time goes on, pay attention to the future uses of magnetic force and remember a thing to ponder – **it is the answer!**

I have always had an inquisitive mind as to how and why things are or work as they do. For example, as a kid, I questioned why the man on the moon is always facing us. It's because it rotates at the same speed as the Earth. In the third grade, I learned the Earth rotates at eight miles a minute. I figured if I jumped up, the Earth would go out from underneath me and move me ¼ mile down the street in a second. But it didn't work as I thought because of my momentum being the same speed. Took me a while to figure this out, but I was in the third grade. Have you ever wonder that all the religions of the world have documented the great flood? So, I have to believe that it actually happened. Have you ever thought about how that could have happened? My theory is that a large meteor slammed into the Atlantic Ocean and sent a 10,000-foot tidal wave on shore and washed civilians out to sea. Then because of the water vapor expelled on impact, it rained for 40 days and 40 nights.

Here is another theory. You have heard of plate tectonics where the North American continent separated from Africa and move 2000 miles across the Atlantic. Why did it do that? The rocks do the slow dance. After much thought, I think the reason it did that was because a billion years ago, our wheel was out of balance and the Earth had a huge wobble that caused the plates to shift to a balanced position.

While pondering the universe I think we have a lot of audacity or ignorance to think that we are the only beings in the universe when there are more stars (suns) than there are grains of sand on the Earth and we're the only ones? REALLY? I believe that we are not ALONE. We have come further in the last 70 years than we have in the pervious 2,000 years. Why do you think that is?

I believe the crash in 1947 in Roswell, New Mexico was the real deal. I believe the government used NASA and the moon shot to fund and cover the reverse engineering of that technology. That brings us to where we are today. Exciting and scary at the same time. I am fortunate to have grown up in one of the best generational times.

The Patch

While Dad was in Gramercy Court, I had flown down to Los Angles to pick up his Mercedes for him because he was giving it to his sister Margaret. I drove it to Sacramento and took it to him. When I walked into his room he said, "Hey, I signed up for hospice today." I said, "Oh good. Did they put a morphine patch on you?" He said, "What kind of patch?" I said, "Excuse me, a Fentanyl patch." He said, "Yes, that's it. I don't want any of that morphine stuff." I said, "Ok."

Three days later the staff was going to take the patch off and put a new one on, but my dad was concerned about his medicine, what it was and what it was going to do. Was it going to be another 72 hours? And nobody could answer his questions. He got the hospice gal on the phone and he got frustrated with the nurses and staff while talking to the hospice woman. I wasn't supposed to ever interrupt my dad when he was on the phone because he'd get angry.

But I said, "Dad, Dad. I can explain it to you." He politely told the hospice lady to hold on. Then he looked at me and sternly said, "Try me." I said, "Dad, three days ago, they brought you a fifth of Jack Daniels and they had given you a half a shot every hour. They now have you to a 3.0 and the bottle is empty. They are bringing you a new bottle with the new patch." He picked up the phone and told the hospice lady, "I understand perfectly. Thank you."

My dad was a recovering alcoholic and sober for 25 years.

Because of the aggressiveness of the cancer and humane assistance of hospice, he passed away a week and half later. Both my wife Sandy's dad and my dad died within one day of each other. Dad was a spiritual man and the Lord said to him "Bill, you're out of money and it's time to go." He could not have timed it any better. He had just enough money to pay his debts and be buried with class. He did it his way and I loved him.

Stress

With no factual basis, I believe stress is a big killer. I picture that we all have these cells that travel all over the body carrying inside cancerous troops that are harmless inside the cell, but when the body is under stress, the whole body starts to tighten up and can squeeze the cells until they pop, sending bad cancerous troops into the body that then find a spot to set up and begin the infestation. I believe Dad's money problems along with marriage problems caused by the shortage of money and his refusal to change his high-finance lifestyle led to his cancer cell bursting and creating his aggressive bone cancer.

Shortly after Dad's death, I sold the office building and closed down the construction office. I went into residential investments. The reason I sold the office is because if there was a financial downturn, I did not have the cash bucket to hold it up and I could lose the whole thing. Too many eggs in one basket. It was time to unload the wagon so we could move forward, which I did. I closed the office, reinvested in residential, married Sandy then built some spec homes and bought some rental properties.

We got whacked in 2008 so we had to unload the wagon again, take the loss to stop the bleeding and move forward. The bear and the bulls get through the forest while the pigs wallow in the mud. Since then, we have made good on the losses. "It's never quite as good or quite as bad as you really think it is."

I could have continued. I had made a decent living in the general contracting business that afforded me more wants and things, but my life direction was changing. Yes, I could still be working and making more money, driving expensive cars, living in a big house, but why? As I mentioned, I don't even like big houses. I have everything I need and more. I had worked hard and accumulated enough assets to provide a modest but good living. What more do I need? It was time to enjoy all my various interests and life: my wife, duck hunting, family, all of the people and friends at the primitive skills gatherings, and freedom to travel and explore new projects like writing this book.

Mom developed Alzheimer's and Sandy took the reins for her caregiving and did a terrific job; I could not have done it, let alone the compassion she gave her. Mom died five years later after three years with Alzheimer's. Alzheimer's is such an awful condition and we definitely need to have a right to terminate life in these conditions. Hell, you would not put your dog through it! Because my mom had it, I have added do not feed or help with drinking on my health instructive for non-resuscitation. Because once you pass the line of doing it yourself, no one can help you, not even Hospice, unless they can prove pain.

Once my quality of life is gone, I do not want to stay around any longer. This reminded me of Dad at Grammercy Court. I remember on one visit as I got to his room, he was rolling down the hallway. When he got settled in his room, I said, "Where did you go?" He said, "I went down to the Alzheimer's meeting." I said, "How was that?" He leaned forward in his chair and pointed his finger at me as he did all the time and said, "They ought to shoot them and put them out of their misery." And I agree.

ATTITUDE

I have always had a positive attitude. The two words I like least are "I can't." Sandy says to me all the time, "You can't do that," and I say, "Yes, I can." She says, "Oh you can do it because you're Tom Cook." And I say, "Yes, that is correct." Then, with some adjustments, I do it in most cases. Positive attitude. Apply the ant theory to "I can't" – you go over it, around it, under it, or through it.

Try blocking a traveling line of ants with an obstacle and watch how they resolve that problem. I have always had a "can-do" attitude towards life, which is probably why I dislike "the I can't." It goes way back to my childhood thought of **"tomorrow will be a better day."**

To illustrate my can-do attitude, when I was in high school, I wanted to take my girlfriend to San Francisco for a really nice French dinner. We got all dressed up, suit and tie, and went to the restaurant. Upon opening the menu, I realized I didn't have enough money to stay in this fancy expensive restaurant. It occurred to me that we CAN'T stay, and I am going to have to tell her we have to leave! Instead, I excused myself from the table and went to the maître d' and said, "I brought my girlfriend from Sacramento to your fine restaurant, but I only have $28.55 cents (a lot of money at the time). I need $1.50 for parking and the bridge, can you do a dinner for two, including tip for $27.00?? I think he was impressed with my moxie. He said yes and put on a show to boot, starting with hors d'oeuvres. Caesar salad made at the table then pheasant under glass for the entrée and then I think crème brulee for dessert.

Another time, I had taken my first wife Haley and my mom to Disneyland and when we arrived, we discovered that the park was closed for some corporation's party. I was a little bummed and said I was going to go see if I can get us in. They said sure how are you going to do that? "I do not know but I will be back." I returned about a half hour later with three tickets and said, "Let's go to the park." How did you do that? (because I'm Tom Cook and have a can-do attitude). I found out who was renting the park, then I went to "will call," gave them my name and got the tickets. You don't give up when you run into an "I can't" situation. Some of this can-do attitude came from the "knock you down to build you up" pep talk about a better way of handling a situation when I had stolen the nuts, bolts and washers from Billby's Hardware store. If you ask, most people are more than willing to help and work with you; you just need to ask. Worst case is they say no! You don't hit any home runs unless you swing at the ball.

I have been on this earth 74 years so far and there is no way I am that old. I'm just not! Maybe 53 in my attitude, like in Toby Keith's song "Don't Let the Old Man In." "How old would you be if you did not know when you were born?" About 53. Maybe. Unfortunately, the body tells me all the time that I am actually 74.

I was telling my friend Chris King about my attitude of being 53 and he gave me his "what are you talking about gaze." Then He said, "Have you looked in the mirror lately?" I fell to the ground laughing because he was right.

Joys of Teaching

The joy I get from teaching the duck processing classes at the primitive skills gatherings is priceless. The kids that take the class year after year—from little Bobby Ray and Zack to Dimitri, Moses, Cree and Garnet, just to name a few of the kids—I get to watch them grow. One of these kids, a boy named Zack Gray, has been picking ducks with me since he was 5 or 6 and is now 12. He is my fire man, because for years he gets the morning fire going for me. He is so efficient; he picked 6 ducks to everyone else's one duck last year. I am going to have to recruit him to be one of my assistants, another duckman junior.

Some years ago at Winter Count, I met another young boy of 10 at the time named Nico Parisi, and he spent the entire week with me. The enjoyment I get from these kids is immeasurable. We did the duck processing, then the next day had a big 100-duck roast over the fire, duck scalps and then duck soup on Thursday. I met his mom Sonia and she told me that Nico had taken my duck picking class the year before and up to that point, he wouldn't touch a fish. Afterward, all he could talk about was Duckman Tom and then again on their way to the next year's event. While talking with Sonia, she asked if I was going to go to the Acorn gathering and I said, "Yes." Then she said she could get a ticket, but the kids' program was already full and Nico could not go. I said, "I bet I can do something about that." Nico said, "How can you do that?" I said, "Because I have a positive attitude," and I teasingly said, "and because I'm Tom

Cook! And how would you like to go as my assistant." Sonia said, "Wow, that would be great."

I had previously arranged with the Acorn gathering leaders Gabriel and Luna to have my own fire to cook the ducks and have my van in my camp and have the designated smoking area at the far end of the village. When we met later at the Acorn gathering, Nico was my assistant. He said, "You can't have your van down here in your camp." I said, "Yes I can." "How?" he asked. Kiddingly, I said, "Because I am Tom Cook." Then he said, "How did you get your own fire?" I again said kiddingly, "Because I am Duckman and we need it for the duck roast and I got permission. I said, "There are ways of getting around the "I can'ts." ASK! Later, he said there was no smoking at Acorn, and I said, "Yes there is because I have arranged for this to be the designated smoking area." I teased him all week with what a positive and CAN-DO attitude can accomplish.

Then later in the week, it was almost dinnertime and I had given my plate to my friend Missy who headed for the food line. I told Nico to get his plate. He said I'll be a couple of minutes – don't wait too long. I went to dinner and joined Missy toward the front of the line and we got our dinner quickly. Well, Nico dallied a few minutes and when he showed up, we were already seated eating and the line had gotten much longer. He said, "How did you get your food so fast??" I said, "Because I am Tom Cook. Plan ahead, make arrangements, ask!"

Another time, I met a young boy from Israel named Pele at Rabbitstick. He only spoke Hebrew and he had fun watching the ducks and everything else that was going on. Then months later, we met up again at Winter Count, and he had picked up some English. He took my duck picking class but left his duck on the stick over the fire. I said, "Pele, how come you didn't eat your duck?" His dad said it was because he is vegetarian. So, the next day I was roasting about 75 ducks over the fire for the camp and Pele came by and watched me. I pointed to the duck and then my tongue motioning "do you want a taste?" He looked at his dad who said if you want to, try a taste. I cut off a large chunk of the beast and gave it to him. He ran off and a couple hours later he came running across the camp right up to me and said, "Duckman—GOOD DUCK" and then ran away. I learned that after returning to his homeland, he was no longer vegetarian.

Melt My Heart

One year at Winter Count, three little girls, 4 maybe 5, just loved the Duckman: Rose, Grace and Iris. One morning, while standing in the middle line working towards breakfast serving tables and talking, these three little girls came up between the lines, stopped right in front of me and said, "Duckman, can we have a hug?" Wow, made my day and brought joy to my heart and the lines on both sides just went oh-ooo. It made their day also.

It's moments like those above and the time I get to spend with Zack and Nico and all the other kids year after year that tap my nurturing button, the one I have not been unaware of most of my life. I think it had to do with the way I was raised in a dysfunctional home with monetary love and no real nurturing. Although I have always been there for my kids, it has not been in a nurturing way, just like my dad. It is partly because I didn't experience it at home and didn't really know what it is or felt like or how to be a nurturing person. That has been slowly changing with my marriage to Sandy and exposure to all the people and the kids that I get to know and watch grow at the gatherings. It has taught me a little bit about what nurturing is and feels like. I am not dead yet and all I can do is recognize and work on it.

Little Nico has really pushed that button in that he wants to be with me and learn. The positive feeling it gives me feeds my soul. So excited, he has already taken and passed his hunter safety course and wants me to take him duck hunting despite living 500 miles away in southern California. He is a determined and excited young man, and we will make it happen. I think this may be a long-term friendship. Like the James Taylor song, "Shower the people—," once you tell somebody the way you feel, you can see it begin to grow. I think it's true about the squeaky wheel always getting the grease. "Show them the way you feel;" but it's a two-way street. You can't make someone love you if they don't.

It occurs to me that in addition to attitude and balance, people and the positive impact they have on one's life are really important. Relations friends and family are important and feed your inner being. I have met so many wonderful people over the years in life and at the gatherings. One year, I was going to Rabbitstick and stopped at a coffee shop in town before going into camp. The restaurant only had a few people and I asked a couple if they were going to Rabbitstick. Surprised that I would know, they said yes and that it was the first time as they had never been before. I told them they were in for the greatest week of their life. This is when I met Rosemary and Mike Wells. Mike asked me, "How did you know we were going to Rabbitstick." I said the tepee pole on your truck gave you away. During that week, we became friends and that was 20 years ago. Wonderful people.

Another time, I was doing a class on duck head scalps and a lady walked up and said, "Can I join the class?" I said, "Sure, hold on to the duck bill while I cut up the neck to the bill." When complete, I flipped the scalp over the head like turning a sock inside out. The problem was it was a head shot and so the skin was bloody red. Well, her eyes got big and she took a couple steps back with this terrified look on her face. I said to her, "What's your name?" "Amy," she said. I said, "Amy, come here." As she got close, I leaned forward and whispered in her ear, "This may not be the class for you." She agreed and thereafter we became friends.

Lotta and Me at Rabbitstick
Photo: Les Corey

One time after four years of friendship, I was sitting on a log with my friend Lotta having one of our many great conversations when I asked her why she, a talented sharp, good-looking woman, did not have a significant other. She said, "Simple, I haven't found the right guy!" Two years later, she shows up with Kent. They are now married 13 years and I get to watch and learn from these two love doves how to improve my own relations. Love and respect for each other!

I could write 30 more pages on the meeting of all the friends and wonderful people over the years. But as another example, some five years ago, I was at Winter Count and it was mid-week when it started raining just before dinner. I said to myself, "Darn it. I didn't bring any rain gear." But then I remembered that Sandy had an umbrella behind the passenger seat. I grabbed the umbrella and went up to get my dinner. After getting dinner, I went to the log pile where I normally sat. As I approached, a lady was sitting on the log by herself in the rain. So I sat down right next to her, put the umbrella up over our heads and said, "Would you like to eat your dinner under my umbrella? Hi, my name is Tom Cook." "What's your name?" "Sarah Pike." Well, she had just arrived for the first time at the event in the dark and in the rain. I told her she had landed in the right spot, as the first time can be overwhelming, and we have been friends ever since. Again, friends and acquaintances are I believe very important to you and your own well being.

I found Rabbitstick 30 years ago and I have only missed one for a wedding in Hawaii. So, it is obvious it was important to me. Sandy said, "Now when we go to Hawaii, are you going to have Rabbitstick withdrawals?" I said, "Probably." But I didn't. It is so difficult to convey the humanity and acceptance that takes place. It is refreshing and it's too bad the world can't work in the same way. But as my friend Patrick Farneman says, we can do it for a week. I have tried to convey the impact that the gatherings and people have had on all who join the family year after year. It is easier to understand when experiencing it first hand. I have been trying to get my friend Charley Meir to go with me for the past 26 years and finally got him to go to Winter Count. I picked him up at the airport and drove to camp in the dark. Then the next morning, looking over the incredible desert landscape, we walked around camp for a bit. He looked at me and said, "Really?" I said, "Really." He had the greatest week of his life and now he was hooked, as is the case with many newcomers. The humanity and acceptance is wonderful to experience. and it was a big impact on my life.

FINALE

Wow, did I make mistakes in my life? Yes, all kinds of mistakes, bad choices and failures in life that cost me dearly and knocked me down tough life lesson learned the hard way. School of hard knocks. Sometimes it's surprising I survived it all. I am not sure where my survival tenacity comes from, but as Dad said, "If you get knocked down, get up and try again." Which I did many times, but there were times, as much as I pulled on my bootstraps, I just could not get myself up, but "tomorrow will be a better day." I kept pulling.

One time in particular, I was a mess and falling apart. My life was uncontrollable. Nothing was working and this was all exacerbated by the drinking and cocaine. I had an important weekend business meeting to go to and I was sobbing and not at all in shape for this meeting. I wasn't drunk but I was an emotional wreck, and I didn't know what to do. Well, like Dad said, "Pray for a parking space," and "more will be revealed."

So, I went to mass, not having been for over 20 years. It was really strange because it was in English and not Latin, which was in my head. I took my act of contrition in the pew and took communion. Mass ended and, still much troubled, I walked to my car with a bewildering fog in my head where nothing computed. I still knew I had to do my best to get ahold of my emotions enough for the meeting. I headed toward that meeting, praying and hoping I could get control before arriving. On the way, driving over the J Street bridge, this column of heat the size of my body rose straight up out of my body, as best as I can describe it, and my sobbing stopped immediately. Was I forgiven? I gained my composure and the meeting went well. It wasn't too long after this that I started in earnest to stop drinking, which took many years to accomplish.

The dysfunctional environment caused by Dad's alcoholism metastasized in many negative ways and led to the destruction of the family unit and relations. Abandonment, greed and, later, favoritism were all based on and rooted in money and power, leading to control and manipulation. I believe that had I not found a different path, I probably would not be here today. I was fortunate that I listened to the sermons, despite them being sometimes boring to a young person. , especially when delivered drunk. I think they were a big help in surviving all the gut-wrenching emotion, anger and rage that permeated my life for a long time.

Along the way, I have picked up and developed my own quips that I combine with Dad's. "Every form of refuge has its price" (Eagles), "It's not on your plate," "Your best efforts got you here" (Gene Duffy), "Whatever you think is best" (Don Ekstrome), "Don't sweat the small shit," "I have no problem with your work as long as it is prefect," and "let me show you a trick I learned in the old country" (Mark Ures), "Be careful what you wish for, you may get it." "If you really need it, a stick will probably do it for you." And many more. These quips can be applied to almost any life situation and difficulty.

Life is sometimes difficult and everyone has their book and experiences to write, and I encourage you to do so. My journey with this book was quite revealing, and I believe it has and will continue to help me because of the clearer understanding and forgiveness, which has lifted the negative weight of the past and brought me a positive outlook of my life. This book required my acknowledgment of the RAGE that burned inside me for years, surfacing on occasions only to be pushed back down with "tomorrow will be a better day." I didn't recognize the depth I carried until I wrote this book, resulting in a letting go of anger and my better understanding of forgiveness and the release it gave me.

While working on this book, I read Mitch Albom's book For One More Day. In it, he asked the question, "If you could change things in your life, would you do it?" Well, my immediate answer is yes, there are all kinds of things I could change. But after thinking about it for a while, I decided I would not change a thing because that's what made me who I am today and I like who and where I am despite all my failures, mistakes and missteps; I am definitely not perfect. What if you could change things? Be careful what you wish for, you might get it. How would the dominos fall if you had made that change? How would my dominos have fallen if I had been 50/50 partners with my brother in the WITH Corporation? I don't think it would have been a good thing, because I would not be who I am today.

While writing, the importance of nature and backpacking, resurrected when I went on the Sierra trek at age 30, became clear to me. Thus began a slow life-changing journey that led me to wanting to learn primitive skills and then led to my family of friends, mentors and teachers at Rabbitstick and Winter Count who helped me change my life direction. I touched on the primitive skills gatherings in an attempt to explain the transformation it sparked over the last 30 years. It is difficult to describe the enlightenment and knowledge I absorbed by participating year after year grounded in reality with the lives of real people from all walks of life who are happy and smiling. The people, their happiness and smiles made me look at my own unhappiness and were the catalyst in changing my perspective from what I had been taught—WORK WORK WORK for more and more! Why? I have all that I need.

How would you like to go to a family reunion where you cannot wait to see hundreds of your friends who love you and you love them? It is a family week of hands-on learning, a week of acceptance, humanity and friendship. The skills connect you to man's basic needs and knowledge taught by experts in their fields. The people and humanity feed the soul and help ground you, at least it does me.

Another saying I touched on, several times throughout the book, was "in the wilderness (outdoors), you are free." You're free of the pressures of everyday life and surrounded by nature's grandeur grounding you to her energy, teachings and wisdom, if you visit enough and learn to be still. This was evident to me on my first packing trip at 12 years old and is just another one of those nature teaching moments. Even then as a kid, I felt free.

Out away from the city lights surrounded by the beauty of a location where your basic needs are in your pack and you are free at least for the moment, free from the bills, work, pressure, the phone and computer. The stress of everyday life fades away momentarily while you sit under a blue sky on a slick rock listening to the sounds around you. Where the invisible teachings and clear view of life can be absorbed while in her serenity. It's a good feeling to be free of the burdens of life that were too heavy to carry, but it made me recognize that I was not free because of the excessive, unnecessary burden caused by too many wants, making it clear that the weight and stress it caused needed to be eliminated.

One thing for certain is that a good attitude is most important in life's situations. Without it, you will be troubled. In a survival situation, a bad attitude will kill you. I used to go on 3-4-day survival exercises at the duck club with only a knife and the clothes on my back to experience and learn. During one, I made my shelter, but went foraging instead of completing the door to the shelter. I got cold, didn't sleep well and got up tired. I went in search of food and materials, and cray fish hunting was unsuccessful. Then it was hot, and I was hungry, tired, dirty and hot. I had a bad attitude and I started complaining out loud to myself! I said, "What are you complaining about, this is survival? It's not supposed to be fun, especially on the first day." Then I said, "The animals aren't complaining. Well, what are they doing? They are taking a nap." I went and found a shady spot, took a nap and woke up with a whole new positive attitude.

I believe second, after attitude, would be balance. Balance is something I have always lacked until my wife Sandy brought it to my life, sometimes too much, but that's not going to hurt me unless I buck too hard, which I do from time to time, causing trouble. Welcome to the Tom and Sandy show. It's hard to believe that I am now in the fourth quarter of life with no idea where or when the 2-minute warning is, but the world keeps turning and life's adventures and challenges are still to be experienced; I plan to make the best of time remaining. I hope my attitude of being 53 keeps me going for a long time.

Although I have used Dad's quips along with my own for years, it was not until I wrote this book that I saw how much influence both parents had on my life. Both good and bad, positive and negative, we all make mistakes. It also made it clear that Mom's guardian angel has always been with me—so listen to your angel. Dad's quips are one way I can share him with others.

If I can pass anything on to the younger people, it is to be conservative and balanced. Make smart choices, plan and be patient for what you need or want, work toward it by saving, then buy what you need and pay cash. The savings on the interest alone is a lot and can be eliminated by being patient and paying cash. Example, maybe you want an expensive BMW but you buy a used, less expensive car first that takes care of your needs. Then, as if you just bought the BMW you wanted with a loan, save that amount each month until you can pay cash.

I thought about all the wasted money I spent on fast, costly cars, big houses and an expensive lifestyle plus the interest payments for those things I didn't really need but had to carry. All that expense could have been saved and invested for later in my life, like now. You're not always going to be in the top 10, so save for later. The grasshopper and the ant. I watch these young men driving the fancy cars just like I did and think to myself—if they only knew.

Don't get me wrong, I am not saying it's a bad thing to be successful and congratulations, if you are. But don't overload your pack, like I did. What I am saying is that there is more to life than work even though I was taught that you WORK, WORK, WORK to make more and more. How much is enough? EVERY FORM OF REFUGE HAS ITS PRICE. What are your interests, hobbies, and desires? It's important to carve out time for those things that bring you joy and happiness. Life is too short.

I made the mistake of not realizing this until I was much older. I had been in pursuit of the success and the almighty dollar and actually paid a fairly high price in that pursuit. Thank God for the teachings of my family of people at the primitive skills gatherings and nature that helped make clear the difference between NEEDS AND WANTS.

Overloading my pack evolved into "unload the wagon to move on." Don't be the Donner party and stay with your stuff until the storm passes. They died for their stuff. They were snowbound; can't go back, can't go forward with the wagon. But they had everything they needed to unload the wagon, hide the items not needed to move forward and take the loss in hopes of retrieving it in the summer. They had food, equipment and shelter canvas. They had tools to make snowshoes and sleds. They had animals that could be processed if they were unable to travel on the path. Had they done that, I believe many more would have survived.

I had a similar experience with the real estate crash of 2007-08. The debt was too high, causing negative cash flow drain on the principal cash. I was bleeding badly and that could not be sustained for long. So, I unloaded the wagon, took the loss and short sold the properties and paid the taxes. Big loss, but it stopped the bleeding and allowed me to move forward. Had I not done that, I would not have moved forward and made up the loss. I could have lost it all. I had to unload the wagon a couple times.

Also, from backpacking and nature, I learned life is similar to backpacking in that it is a solo and personal journey even though there are people around. It is completed in the world around you; it has pain, strain, and pleasure; it has its ups and downs and its difficult spots to overcome; it has its stormy and sunshine days. It makes it clear when you're going too fast or carrying too much weight, or not doing what is needed. It clearly defines the difference between needs and wants and points out that you do not need much except for the basics, which again is sometimes out of view in life unless recognized. The lesson learned turned into a better understanding, wisdom and quips "don't overload your life's pack," be patient, you will get there one step at a time. Plan and map your trip through life as you would a backpacking trip. Have a great life.

Believe in your God, be good to yourself, be good to your neighbor and smile. Now, I want to run for president (watch for my next book)!

Reviews

Reviews are very much appreciated.

To write a review, please find the book on Amazon and scroll to the bottom of the page.

Click on "customer review," log into Amazon and choose a star rating, Write a review and click submit. It will show your review.

In gratitude.

Made in the USA
Middletown, DE
03 September 2024